Pitman 2000 Shorthand

# Rapid Review
# and Speed Development

BRYAN COOMBS

Addison Wesley Longman Limited
Edinburgh Gate, Harlow
Essex CM20 2JE, England
*and Associated Companies throughout the world*

First published in Great Britain 1991
Reprinted 1993, 1994
Reprinted by Longman Group Limited 1995
Reprinted 1996

**British Library Cataloguing-in-Publication Data**
A catalogue entry for this title is available from the British Library.

ISBN 0-582-29170-4

**Library of Congress Cataloging-in-Publication Data**
A catalog entry for this title is available from the Library of Congress.

Printed in Singapore.

# Contents

# How to use this book

## Theory revision

Revise the theory by working through the rules and examples set out in each unit.

Start at the beginning, if you wish, and proceed through to the last unit. You may want to revise in an order which is different to the book presentation; the choice is yours.

Become familiar with the rules. You do not have to know them by heart, but you must know them well enough to apply them.

The material which immediately follows the theory section is useful for testing your ability to apply the rule which is being revised. Read and rapid-read the passage and then take it from dictation several times.

## Short forms, phrases and intersections

These are spread throughout the book and are generally connected with the theory being revised. To give a balance to the number of these special outlines being revised in each unit, you will find that some of them are not directly linked to the particular theory of the unit in which they appear.

You must know these outlines so well that you can write them instantly on hearing them. Together with the 700 common words (listed at the end of this book) they form the foundation of your shorthand skill. Without complete mastery of them you cannot expect to progress. Drill them in the groups presented until you feel you have them under control.

Use the exercise material, which follows each new group of these special outlines, to test your knowledge. Rapid-read the passage, which contains many of the short forms and phrases, and take it from dictation. Repeat the reading and the dictation several times.

## Skill development

These sections are presented to assist you in the development of your shorthand skill. The advice is based on many years of experience, and combines the author's practical shorthand writing in the courts with his teaching of shorthand. This same advice has helped students throughout the world, and it can help you, too.

## Speed development

Writing speed develops through:

- Having a working knowledge of the rules and applying them to write correct outlines without hesitation.
- Knowing all the short forms and intersections.
- Having a solid foundation of basic outlines, the 700 common words, on which to develop a working business vocabulary.
- Being familiar with all the phrasing principles and being able to apply them.
- Being able to read printed shorthand, and your own notes, as quickly as if you were reading a typed page.

These five points are made possible through:

1  **Identifying** those outlines which require special attention, as a result of hesitancies when reading shorthand, or finding errors when checking shorthand notes.

2  **Drilling** outlines which have caused hesitancy in reading or writing. This means writing single outlines, or phrases, many times until mastered (there is no set magic number which guarantees success). Always write as quickly as you can, and say the word(s) to yourself as you write. Vary the technique. Write, say, 12 outlines you wish to drill on the first line of a notebook and then fill each line of the page with the same outlines. If any outline from those 12 is still causing a problem, fill a whole page with that outline.

3  **Rapid reading** of printed shorthand and your own notes. The faster you can read shorthand, the faster you can write it. Take any passage of shorthand and check how many seconds it takes you to read it. Make a note of the time taken. Then drill any outlines which caused you to hesitate. Repeat the reading, aiming for a much faster reading time; note how long it takes. Repeat these steps until you can read the whole passage without any hesitancy.

Bryan Coombs

# New short forms

| | | | |
|---|---|---|---|
| advantage | | impossible | |
| advertise/advertisement | | inconvenience/incon-venient/inconveniently | |
| advertised | | indifferent | |
| advertising | | insurance | |
| behalf | | maximum | |
| character | | minimum | |
| characteristic | | misrepresent | |
| different/difference | | November | |
| differently | | number | |
| disadvantage | | opinion | |
| during | | opportunity | |
| everything | | principle/principal/principally | |
| February | | represent | |
| financial/financially | | representation | |
| general/generally | | representative | |
| however | | significance | |
| importance/important | | signify/significant | |
| importantly | | | |

viii

| | |
|---|---|
| sure | ⌇ |
| unusual/unusually | ⌇ |
| usual/usually | ⌇ |

## New intersection

| | |
|---|---|
| morning | ⌒ |

# Acknowledgement

The author wishes to express his appreciation to Jane Robinson for her expert guidance and encouragement in the preparation of this manuscript.

# UNIT 1
## Position writing, diphthongs, triphones and diphones

## Position writing

The first vowel sound in a word determines the position of the first stroke of an outline.

**First position**: first upward or downward stroke *above* the line

rightly   rapid   far   opposite   attaching

**Second position**: first upward or downward stroke *to* or *from* the line

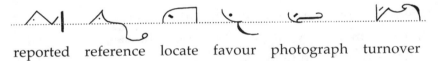

reported   reference   locate   favour   photograph   turnover

**Third position**: first upward or downward stroke *through* the line

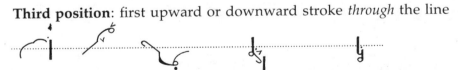

limited   realise   previously   disappointed   dividends

**Horizontal strokes**: When an outline begins with a horizontal stroke, it is the first upstroke or downstroke which is written in the correct position:

actually   unfortunately   movement   international   inquiry

Outlines consisting only of horizontal strokes are written *above* the line for first position and *on* the line for second and third position:

minor   agreement   encountered   economics   intention   quicker

### SKILL DEVELOPMENT

*Correct position writing* is essential for accurate, rapid transcription. Write the first upstroke or downstroke well above the line for first place; to the line for second place; well through the line for third place.

*Diphthongs* must always be inserted.

*Diphones* are essential in certain outlines (such as **area**). Familiarise yourself with those outlines and always use the diphone sign.

## Diphthongs and triphones

The four diphthongs **I, OI, OW** and **U** and triphones (diphthongs plus another vowel, which is indicated by adding a tick to the diphthong sign) should always be inserted. These signs make an outline instantly recognisable and aid transcription.

First position, **I** and **OI**

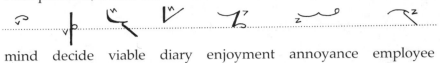

mind   decide   viable   diary   enjoyment   annoyance   employee

Third position, **OW** and **U**

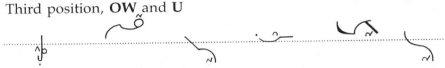

outstanding   allowances   power   communicate   valuable   fewer

## Diphones

Two consecutive vowels are indicated by using a diphone sign, placing it in the position of the first vowel.

Diphones are essential in a few outlines:

area   radio   idea   video   creates   theatre   associate

The diphone is always useful as a transcription aid, but it may be safely omitted in many outlines:

experience   million   material   really   earlier

If ever you have any doubts about omitting the diphone (or any other vowel sign), it is always safer to include it.

## Theory revision drill

### Letter to Miss Jackson about a photocopier

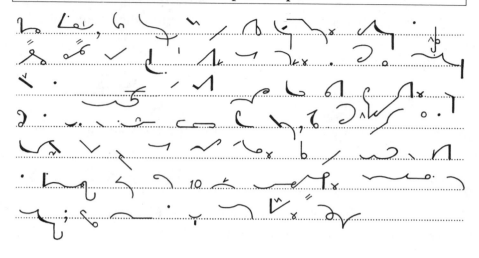

### Key

Dear Miss Jackson, Thank you for your inquiry about our / latest photocopier. We have had an outstanding response as a / result of our advertising on radio in the area. The / machine is manufactured by an international company and already millions / have been sold throughout the world. Today there is a / need to communicate quicker than ever before, and this machine / really has a valuable part to play in the modern / office. It is our intention to hold a demonstration here / from 10 am next Wednesday. I am enclosing your / invitation; please make a note in your diary. Yours sincerely / **(100 words)**

## Short forms

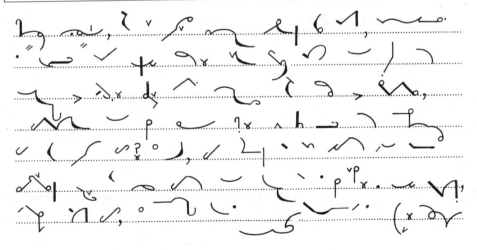

a/an  all  almost  already  although  always  also  altogether

and  be  I  how  it  the  you  usual(ly)  unusual(ly)

## Intersection

D ....|.... department

## Short form and phrasing drill

Letter to Mrs Mason about a sale at a department store

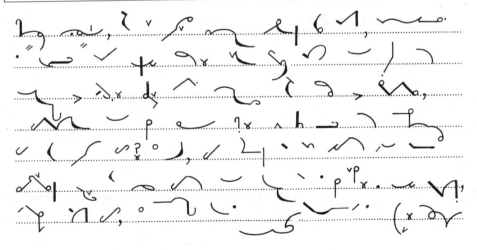

## Key

Dear Mrs Mason, Although I realise you may have received / this already, I am enclosing a photograph of our new / department store. I have pleasure also in attaching your invitation / to the opening. Despite the rapid movement of other stores / to the suburbs, we believe in city centre trading. How / do you give your customers what they really want? As / usual, we asked all of you and were not altogether / surprised to find that most were in favour of a / city site. The new building, opposite the old one, has / accommodation for an international bank and a theatre. Yours sincerely /

**(100 words)**

## CORRESPONDENCE

A letter, a memorandum and a report about a photocopier supplied by International Copiers Limited.

## Letter to the Manager, International Copiers Limited

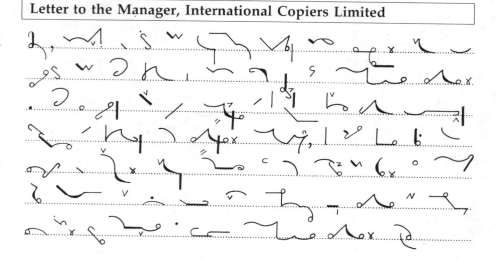

## Key

Dear Sir, I am writing to complain about the photocopier /
purchased almost six months ago. I have no serious complaint /
about the machine itself but I am very disappointed with / the
maintenance service. The machine is used by our Invoice /
Department and at peak times we have encountered problems
and / telephoned your Service Department. Unfortunately, it
always takes days for / someone to arrive. I have had arguments
with your employees / about this. As manager of this bank I aim
to / give my customers good service and I expect the same / of
you. Please organise a quicker maintenance service. Yours
faithfully / (100 words)

---

## Memo
**To: Head of Service Department   From: Manager**
**Subject: Customer complaint**

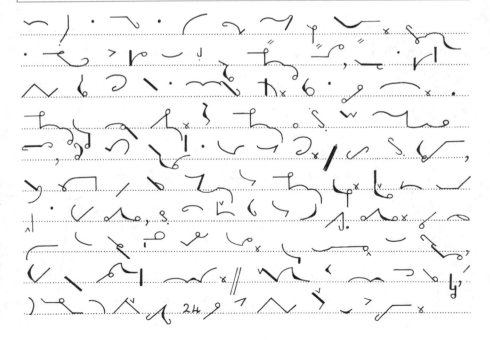

8

## Key

I am attaching a copy of a letter from the / Manager of City Bank. Please let me have an explanation / of the delays in attending to this customer's calls, together / with a detailed report on this machine by a member / of your department. This is a serious matter. The customer's / confidence must be restored. Although the customer is complaining about / the maintenance agreement, there is also obviously a fault in / the machine.

When planning this work, be sure to select / our best engineer for the customer visit. Advise him to / carry out a thorough service, spending more time than for / the usual routine service. He must look for possible causes / of recent faults. If he encounters any problems, they are / to be resolved immediately.

I believe that immediate action pays / dividends, and so I expect your reply within 24 / hours and the report by the end of the week. /

**(150 words)**

## Report on Photocopier Model 700, Serial Number AZ 56789

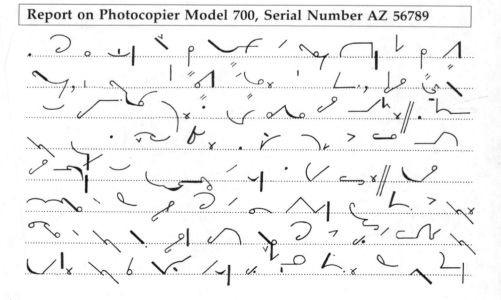

*[Shorthand outlines]*

## Key

The machine is owned by City Bank Limited and presently /
located at the City Road branch, but previously at Head / Office.
On checking, it was found to be in working / order. A full service
was carried out.

The automatic paper / feed required a minor adjustment. The
whole area of the / glass carrier was covered in fingerprints and
needed a thorough / clean.

Various members of staff use the machine and some / reported
frequent jamming of the paper. Samples of paper being / used
were beside the machine and the weight and quality / of the
paper varied. Paper which is below the recommended / weight
causes jamming. Staff should be asked to make reference / to the
guidelines in the handbook about paper to be / used.

An inquiry about machine usage at peak periods revealed /
that the number of copies being made is actually in / excess of
the maximum number recommended for this model. This /creates
a serious heat problem. The automatic safety system cuts / the
power to the motor and the machine stops. Almost / all of the
reported faults have been caused by overheating. /     **(180 words)**

## SPEED DEVELOPMENT

Before you begin this section, read *'How to use this book'* (see page iv).

Now turn to page 5 and the passage which begins, *'Dear Mrs Mason . . .'*.

This letter contains many of the short forms, phrases and intersections reviewed in this unit.

### Your aim

To master short forms and phrases and to be able to write these outlines rapidly to increase your writing speed.

### Your action

1  Read the passage as quickly as you can. Time yourself. There are only 100 words and it should take you less than a minute. Make a note of any outlines which you cannot read, or which cause you to hesitate.
2  Drill those outlines.
3  Repeat steps 1 and 2 until you can read the passage very quickly and without any hesitation.
4  Take the passage from dictation, by having someone read to you, or by recording it yourself on a tape.
5  Repeat the dictation several times but always read through the printed shorthand as quickly as you can before taking the next dictation.

# UNIT 2
## Stroke S and Z; circle S, SES circle; ST and STR loop

**Stroke S** is used:

When **S** is the only consonant in a word, when a word begins **S-vowel-S**, and in derivatives

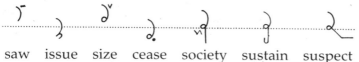

saw   issue   size   cease   society   sustain   suspect

unsuspecting   systematic

**Stroke Z** is used:

When **Z** is the only consonant and when **Z** is the first sound in a word

ease   zero   zone   zealous   Zimbabwe

**Stroke S** or **Z** is used when **vowel-S** or **vowel-Z** begins a word, and when **S-vowel** or **Z-vowel** ends a word:

ascertain   isolate   estimate   easily   policy   agency   busy   plaza

The use of the strokes in the previous examples indicates the presence of a vowel and therefore it is not necessary to insert a vowel sign.

## Circle S

In all other cases the sound of **S** or **Z** is represented by a small circle written inside curves, outside angles and anti-clockwise to straight strokes:

sense   seems   besides   receipt   succeed   decide   speed   sort

## SES circle

The circle represents two S's (or the combination of S and Z) and therefore is large. The **SES circle** should always be large enough to distinguish it from **circle S**.

The sounds **SES**, **SEZ** and **ZES** are represented by a large circle

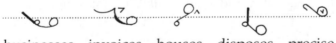

businesses   invoices   houses   disposes   precise

## ST and STR loops

To aid transcription, make a clear distinction between the loops. **ST** is thin and half the length of the stroke to which it is attached; **STR** is fat and two-thirds the length of the stroke to which it is attached:

| story | adjust | standard | start | stimulate | faster | administer |

| investors | toastmaster |

## Theory revision drill

### Letter to Mr Smith

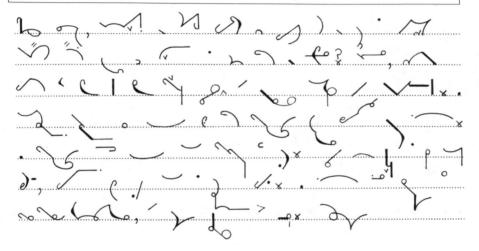

### Key

Dear Mr Smith, I am writing to ascertain whether you / wish us to issue a renewal policy or if you / would like an estimate from two other companies? Of course, / you will be aware that every day several private houses / and businesses in this city are burgled. The unsuspecting public / is under threat from professional thieves as well as the / busy amateur. The professional can enter any property with ease. / He may divide a city into zones, working through each / in a systematic way. The amateur acts speedily as opportunities / present themselves, and easily disposes of the goods. Yours sincerely /    **(100 words)**

## Short forms

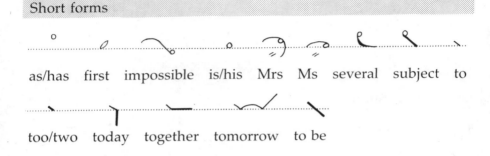

as/has  first  impossible  is/his  Mrs  Ms  several  subject  to

too/two  today  together  tomorrow  to be

## Phrases

**Circle S** is very useful as a link between two outlines, and it also represents the words **is, his, as, has, us, once**:

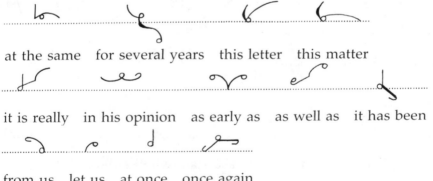

at the same   for several years   this letter   this matter

it is really   in his opinion   as early as   as well as   it has been

from us   let us   at once   once again

## SES circle

This large circle represents **as-s, s-is/has, is/his-s, s-s**

as soon as we can    this is necessary    this has been    it is certainly

this city

## ST loop

This loop is used to join outlines and also represents the word
**first**:

as fast as    just now    last year    at first    very first

The short form **first** is also used in phrases:

first-class    first thing    first of all

## Intersection

**BS** ........ **business**

## Short form and phrasing drill

### Letter to Mrs Long about a typewriter repair

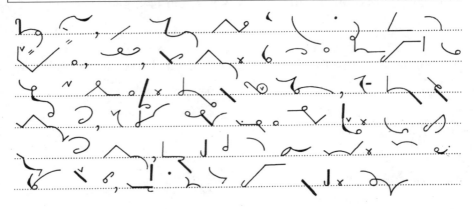

### Key

Dear Mrs Long, Our engineer reports that after a systematic /
check your typewriter is, in his opinion, beyond repair. This /
man has worked for us for several years and I / respect his
judgment. It is impossible to be precise in / this matter, and
though it may be possible to repair / the machine, I think it is
really sensible to accept / his expert advice. If you wish to have
the machine / repaired, it can be done at once or first thing /
tomorrow. I am sending this letter by hand, together with / an
estimate for the work to be done. Yours sincerely /     **(100 words)**

## SKILL DEVELOPMENT

Be consistent in the size of your strokes, circles and loops.

**SES circle** represents the sound of two s's and must be twice the size of the **S circle**.

The **ST loop** is shallow and half the length of the stroke to which it is attached.

**STR loop** is fatter and two-thirds the length of the stroke to which it is attached.

For ease of recognition *exaggerate* the size of the **SES circle** and **STR loop**.

## CORRESPONDENCE

This consists of two letters and a memo between Rapid Printing Limited and The Standard Advertising Agency Limited.

### Letter to the Manager, The Standard Advertising Agency Limited

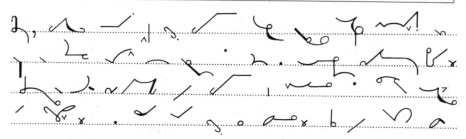

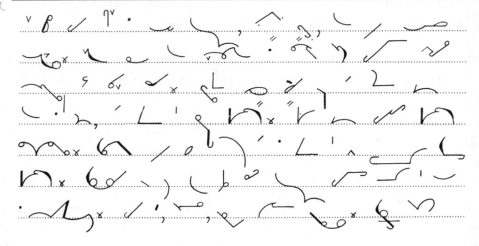

## Key

Dear Sir, We have been carrying out printing work for / several businesses in this city and I am writing to / you today to ask you to allow me to submit / an estimate the next time you require stationery. It is / impossible to show you the range of our work but / I enclose a sample invoice and price list. The standard / of our printing is first-class. It is our policy / first of all to ascertain a customer's requirements, complete the / job as soon as we can and deliver to the / specified address. Why not try our business service? Yours faithfully / **(100 words)**

## Memo
**To: Office Manager   From: General Manager**
**Subject: Stationery printing**

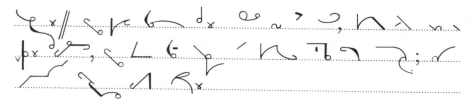

## Key

I suggest we try a new firm, Rapid Printing, for / our next invoices. I have seen for myself a sample / of their work and I was impressed with the high / standard. Please contact Mr Storey today and ask him for / an estimate, and check on speed of delivery. Tell him / we want delivery as early as possible. This will be / our first order and a check on how quickly they / can deliver. This is necessary to see if it is / the sort of firm we can call on in an / emergency. We ought, of course, to support local businesses. This / has been company policy for several years.

Please deal with / this matter at once. As soon as you have all / the information, it will be up to you to decide. / Once again, please check those postal and telephone codes very / carefully; you will recall the problems we had last year. /          **(150 words)**

## Letter to Mr Storey, Manager, Rapid Printing Limited

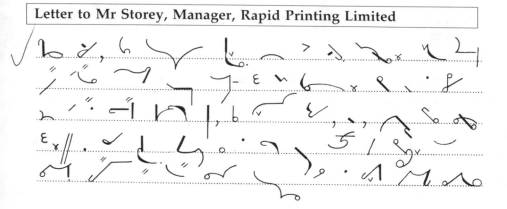

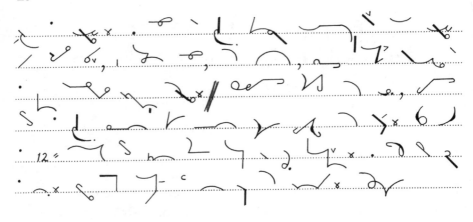

## Key

Dear Mr Storey, Thank you for your letter advising me / of the opening of your business. I have asked our / Office Manager to get in touch with you about this / matter. Subject to a satisfactory estimate and an agreed delivery / date, it is likely that we, too, will be able / to place some business with you.

The Standard Advertising Agency / is a very busy national company which specialises in handling / work for small firms and has a wide range of / services to offer a new business. The costs of advertising / which must be incurred by any new business are always / high, but for the same costs, or lower, you can / enjoy the benefits of a team of experts to promote / your business.

As soon as we can ascertain your needs, / we can plan an advertising scheme which will come easily / within your budget. This is usually a 12-month plan / but you may ask for it to cease at any / time. The very first step would be a meeting. Please / get in touch with me today or tomorrow. Yours sincerely /**(180 words)**

## SPEED DEVELOPMENT

Turn to page 17 and the passage which begins 'Dear Sir, We have been . . .'.

This passage contains 100 words.

### Your aim

To be able to read and write each outline without hesitation.

### Your action

1   Read through the letter and circle with a pencil any outline which causes you to hesitate.
2   Check each encircled outline with the key.
3   Drill these outlines (refer to page vi to see what drilling really means).
4   Re-read the letter several times until you can read it through completely without any hesitation. This is the test. When you can do this it means you really do know the outlines.
5   Take the letter from dictation. Which outlines caused you to hesitate when taking the dictation? Identify these by re-reading the printed shorthand and then drill these outlines. Repeat the dictation at least three times.

# UNIT 3
## Strokes F and V; F/V hook

## Strokes F and V

**Strokes F** and **V** are both scooped-out curves:

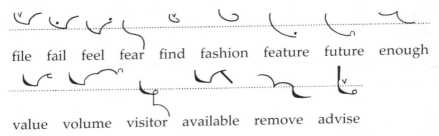

file  fail  feel  fear  find  fashion  feature  future  enough

value  volume  visitor  available  remove  advise

## F/V hook

The **F/V hook** is used only at the end of straight strokes:

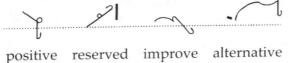

positive  reserved  improve  alternative

**Circle S** may be added to the final hook:

observes  reserves  motives  improves

The **F/V hook** is also used in the middle of an outline:

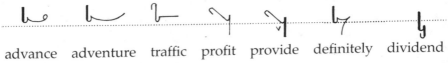

advance  adventure  traffic  profit  provide  definitely  dividend

When a word ends in a vowel, the **stroke F/V** is used. The use of the stroke indicates the presence of a final vowel and there is no need to show it:

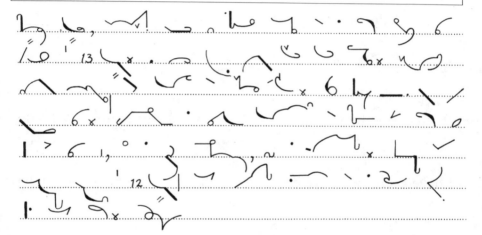

half *but* heavy   serve *but* survey

## Theory revision drill

### Letter to a customer

### Key

Dear Mrs Evans, I am writing to give you advance / notice of a very special sale which commences on 13 / February. The main feature will be fine fashion clothes. I / feel sure you will be impressed by the value of / items on offer. This is definitely going to be our / biggest sale. We expect a heavy volume of traffic on / the very first day of the sale but, as an / established customer, you have an alternative. Take advantage of our / invitation to view on 12 February in the relative calm / of an ordinary shopping day in the store. Yours sincerely / **(100 words)**

## Short forms

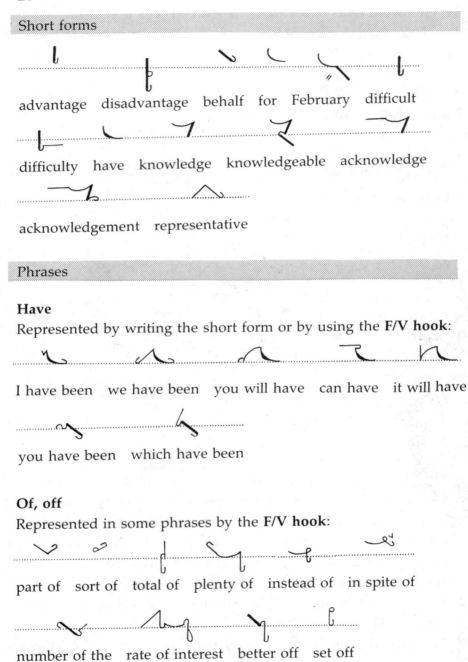

advantage   disadvantage   behalf   for   February   difficult

difficulty   have   knowledge   knowledgeable   acknowledge

acknowledgement   representative

## Phrases

**Have**
Represented by writing the short form or by using the **F/V hook**:

I have been   we have been   you will have   can have   it will have

you have been   which have been

**Of, off**
Represented in some phrases by the **F/V hook**:

part of   sort of   total of   plenty of   instead of   in spite of

number of the   rate of interest   better off   set off

## Intersections

F      ⌒ form

L      ⌒ limited

KL      ⌒ company limited

## Short form and phrasing drill

### Letter from a bank manager

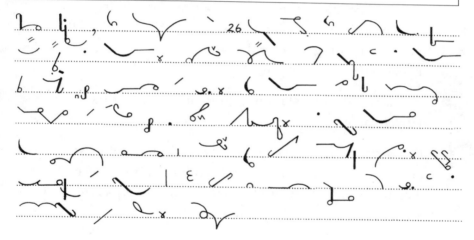

## SKILL DEVELOPMENT

*Vowels, diphthongs and diphones*   Most outlines do *not* require a vowel to enable you to transcribe them at speed and with complete accuracy.

*Strokes and hooks*   The correct use of a stroke rather than a hook indicates the presence of a vowel in an outline, and there is no need to insert the vowel.

*Essential vowels*   Through experience you will learn which outlines do need a vowel and you will place the vowel according to the rules. Rarely does an outline need more than one vowel.

*Half-length outlines* standing on their own must have a vowel shown.

*Proper nouns, names and addresses* should have at least one vowel sign when you first write them in a piece of dictation; when they are repeated within the passage, it is not necessary to write the vowels.

*Diphthongs*   The four diphthong signs, which represent a vowel sound immediately followed by another vowel sound, must always be written. They stand out in your shorthand note and greatly assist transcription.

*Diphones*   In a few outlines the placing of a diphone is essential to aid transcription. Get to know these outlines and always write this important sign in them.

## Key

Dear Miss Davidson, Thank you for your letter of 26 / February explaining that you were having difficulty in choosing a / bank. You will find yourself much better off with a / bank which has knowledge of student incomes and needs. This / bank has the advantage of many years of experience and / offers students the highest rate of interest. A number of / the banks have similar schemes but in spite of these / we are the acknowledged leaders. Please complete the enclosed form / and bring it with you when you come to discuss / your needs with a member of our staff. Yours sincerely / **(100 words)**

## CORRESPONDENCE

This consists of two letters and a memo concerning the General Manager and Sales Manager of City Office Supplies Company Limited, and a prospective client, Mr David Robb.

### Letter to the General Manager, City Office Supplies Company Limited

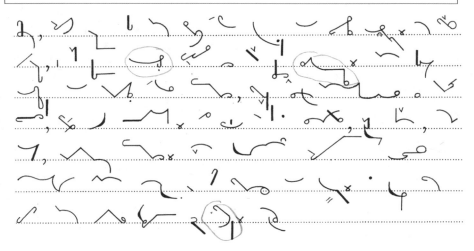

## Key

Dear Sir, I wish to take advantage of your special / offer featured in yesterday's newspaper. Your prices are competitive, but / I had difficulty understanding what was meant by discount certificates. / I am definitely interested in purchasing office equipment provided some / form of maintenance is part of the agreement, plus the / usual guarantee. As the owner of a small business I / do not have the time, or the knowledge, to repair / equipment. My volume of work increases monthly and I am / moving to larger premises in February. A visit from one / of your representatives this week would be appreciated. Yours faithfully /

**(100 words)**

**Memo**
**To: Sales Manager  From: Managing Director**
**Subject: Advertising Campaign**

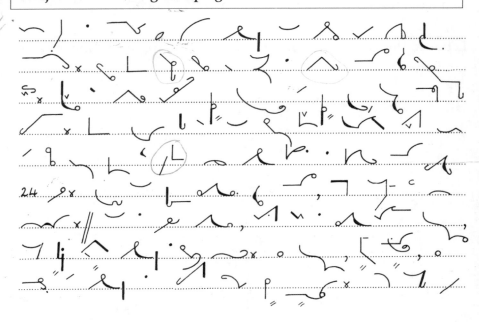

*[shorthand symbols]*

## Key

I am attaching a copy of the first letter received / in response to our latest advertising campaign. Please take positive / steps to ensure a representative calls on this prospective client. / Advise all representatives to reserve Tuesday afternoons and Tuesday evenings / for this extra work. Take full advantage of any spare / time available right now and stress to your team that / each contact must receive at least a telephone call within / 24 hours. If you have any difficulty servicing these / calls, get in touch with me immediately.

In a recent / review, I read about a survey of local firms, in / which David Robb received a special mention. His firm, Top / Fashions Company Limited, is expanding and received an award from / the City Council. Your knowledge of our very competitive field / is enough to ensure this sort of opportunity is not / missed. We have been set targets and must not fail. /     **(150 words)**

### Letter to Mr David Robb, Managing Director, Top Fashions Company Limited

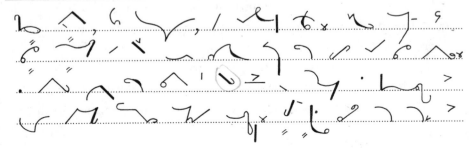

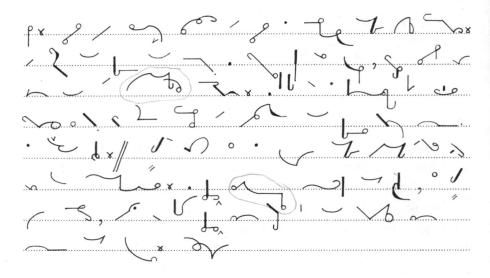

## Key

Dear Mr Robb, Thank you for your letter, which I / received this morning. I have been in touch with the / Sales Manager and by now you will have heard from / one of our sales representatives. The representative will be very / happy on behalf of the company to arrange a demonstration / of the full range of equipment in which you are / interested. John Davis serves your area of the city. He / is our senior salesman and he has an extensive knowledge / of the latest equipment. Should there be any difficulty in / keeping the proposed date of his visit, please do not / hesitate to let him know and alternative arrangements can be / made. The advantage of a demonstration at the owner's premises / is being able to ask questions and resolve any difficulties / before making a final decision.

John also has a full / knowledge of the range of options open to you for / maintenance. The discount certificates mentioned in the advertisement, as John / will explain, relate to additional discounts you may obtain on / any purchases you may make in the future. Yours sincerely /                    **(180 words)**

## SPEED DEVELOPMENT

Turn to page 23 and the passage which begins, *'Dear Mrs Evans . . .'*. This letter contains many examples of the theory being reviewed in this unit.

### Your aim

To master new outlines through rapid reading.

### Your action

First of all, turn to page vi *'How to use this book'* and read paragraph 3. Follow these instructions whenever rapid reading is mentioned.

1   Rapid read the letter, checking the key if necessary.
2   Repeat this reading until all points of hesitancy have been removed.
3   Take the letter from dictation at least 3 times. Make the most of a cassette player if you have one, or persuade someone to dictate to you by reading from the key. In between each dictation, rapid read the printed shorthand.

# UNIT 4
## Stroke R; R hook

When there is an R in the spelling of a word it is always shown in the shorthand outline. Although the R sound is not always pronounced in some words, it ought to be, and for that reason it appears in the outline.

## Stroke R

**Upward R** is written:

When **R** is the first sound in a word, that is at the *beginning* of an outline; in the *middle* of an outline; and at the *end* of an outline when final **stroke R** is followed by a vowel:

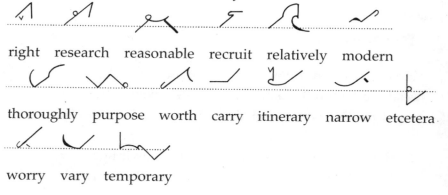

right   research   reasonable   recruit   relatively   modern

thoroughly   purpose   worth   carry   itinerary   narrow   etcetera

worry   vary   temporary

**Downward R** is written:

At the *beginning* of an outline when **R** is preceded by a vowel; at the *end* of an outline when R is the final sound; and *before* **M:**

arrangements   arrival   assure   ordinary   original   were

similar   transfer   form   remain   reminder   ceremony

When **R** at the end of an outline is immediately followed by a circle or loop:

force   course   nurse   resources   worst

In derivatives of root words ending with the downward **stroke R**:

appearance   fairly   warehouse   conference   reference   powerful

Applying the rules for the use of **upward** and **downward R** at the beginning or ending of an outline will indicate the presence or absence of a vowel. Vowels which are indicated in this way can, of course, safely be omitted from the outline, eg were, worry. Writing the correct outline aids transcription and develops speed.

## R hook

**R hook** is written at the beginning of a stroke: inside curves, with a clockwise motion to straight downstrokes and underneath horizontal strokes:

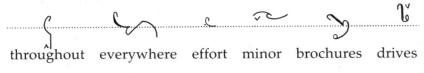

throughout   everywhere   effort   minor   brochures   drives

private    prefer    electronic    major    agreement    credit    increase

**Circle S** is added to straight strokes hooked for **R** by closing the hook, and is read first.

spread    stress    strength    supermarket

**Circle S** is reduced in size and written inside the hook in the middle of an outline (write a tiny circle and then form the hook by an upward movement):

distribution    demonstrate    administrate

**Circle S** is added to a hooked curve by writing a tiny circle first and then extending into the shape of the hook so that both circle and hook show:

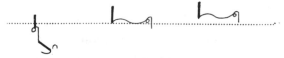

safer    suffer    summer    sooner

**ST loop** is combined with **R hook** by writing the loop first on the **R hook** side:

stagger    sticker    steeper

The sound **Sgr** or **Skr** following strokes **D**, **B** or **P** is represented as follows:

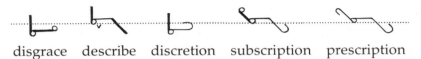

disgrace   describe   discretion   subscription   prescription

**FR**, **VR**, **Thr** and **THR** are reversed after horizontal strokes and upstrokes:

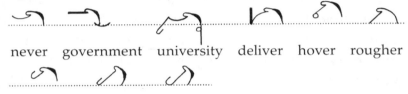

never   government   university   deliver   hover   rougher

whatever   weather   whether

## Theory revision drill

### Letter to Miss Major

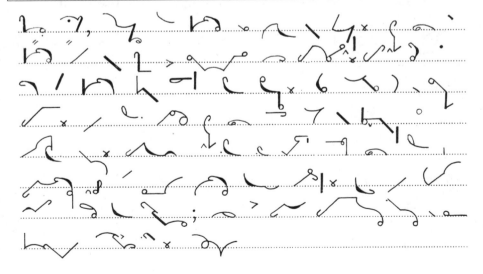

## Key

Dear Miss Major, Arrangements for deliveries to us will have / to
be changed. Throughout the summer all deliveries are to / be
direct to the supermarket's main warehouse. When there is / a
very large delivery it should be staggered over several / days.
This enables us to spread the work. Our staffing / resources
throughout the summer can only be described as relatively /
poor. We have made every effort to recruit extra summer / staff
but university students and school leavers have not responded. /
Even our thoroughly modern stores have problems; most of the /
young workforce appears to seek temporary employment abroad.
Yours sincerely /                                     **(100 words)**

## Short forms

accord/according/according to   accordingly   advertise(ment)

before   dear   during   from   however   more   number   sure

very

## Phrases

**according to the**

## Are

The short form  **are** joins easily to many other outlines. These simple phrases should always be used. Phrasing, the joining together of two or more outlines, is one of the keys to successful speed development.

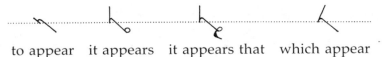

you are   we are   they are   there are   are you

**R hook** is used extensively in phrasing to represent the following words:

## Appear

to appear   it appears   it appears that   which appear

## Course

of course   in the course of the   in due course

## Far

too far   how far   so far   very far   by far the most

## Other (omitting R hook)

any other   no other   many other   on the other hand

38

**Our**

in our   in our view   in our opinion   it is in our interests

**Part**

your part   large part   major part   various parts   in all parts

to take part

    *10*        *10*

**Note:**   10 per cent   10 per cent per annum

Intersection

**Upward R** ⟋ **require/required/requirement**

Short form and phrasing drill

**Memo**
**To: Credit Control Manager**   **From: General Manager**
**Subject: Additional staff**

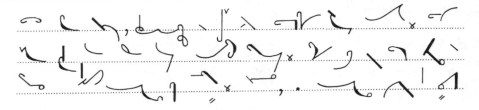

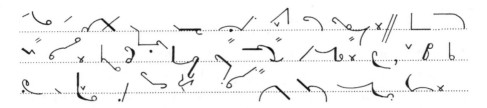

## SKILL DEVELOPMENT

### L and R hooks

Many students are confused about the direction of a
hook and, in particular, do not consistently distinguish
between the **L hook** and the **R hook**. When
transcribing their notes they guess what an outline
represents. Time is too precious in the business world
to spend on guessing. There should be no need to
guess; accurate notes lead to accurate and rapid
transcription.

To resolve this problem, revise the **L hook** section
from the basic theory book, drilling all example
outlines many times. Spend extra study time on the
same section of this book. Revise the **R hook** in the
same way. Drill the examples containing both hooks
many times: **problem, critical, practical**.

## Key

More than ever before, it is in our interests to / tighten up credit control all over the north. Accordingly I / have advertised for staff for each northern branch. There are / sure to be very large numbers of applicants and we / shall interview during October. Of course the interviews will be / at Head Office and you will be required to take / part together with Mary Wright from Personnel.

Take care about / salaries. It appears there is a danger of breaching Government / recommendations. However, I suggest it is safer to advise each / applicant of what the salary will be before interviewing them. /

**(100 words)**

## CORRESPONDENCE

A letter and two memos about the Export Manager's visit to Hong Kong to attend a conference.

## Letter to the Manager, Hong Kong Hotel, Hong Kong (to be sent by fax)

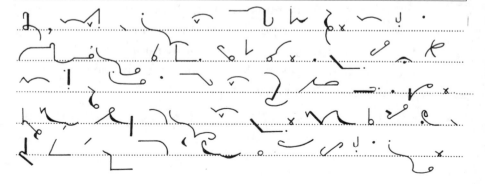

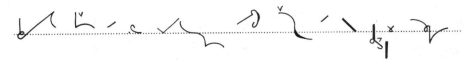

## Key

Dear Sir, I am writing to confirm my accommodation at / the end of this month. I am attending an electronics / conference which is taking place at the hotel. The booking / was made last month and I am adding to this / fax a copy of my original request giving the details. / It appears that I have not received your confirmation of / my booking. I believe it is always safer to double / check and to take care that everything is in order / when attending a conference. It is worth time and effort / to reconfirm rather than arrive and be disappointed. Yours truly / **(100 words)**

## Memo
**To: Branch Manager, Hong Kong   From: Export Manager**
**Subject: Electronics conference   (to be faxed)**

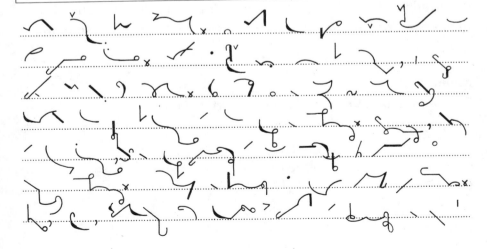

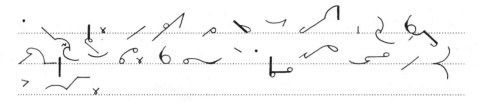

## Key

I will be arriving at the end of the month. / You already have details of my itinerary in last week's / fax. I will require a driver to meet me at / the airport, but please do not worry about being there / yourself. This message is to ensure you have enough brochures / available for distribution at the conference and for visits to / customers. Please make arrangements, before and after the conference, to / visit the university and any government departments which you regard / as potential customers. Arrange to demonstrate a full range of / our equipment. It appears, however, that we have competition from / various parts of the world and it is in our / interests to put on a powerful display. Our research is / the best in the world but so far this has / not been reflected in sales. This is something of a / disgrace and we must increase our share of the market. /     **(150 words)**

**Memo**
**To: Managing Director    From: Export Manager**
**Subject: Hong Kong conference**

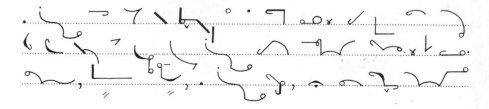

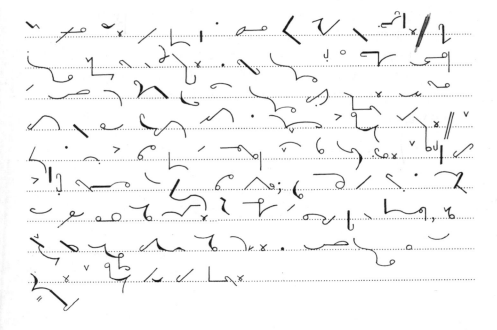

---

**Key**

The conference can only be described as a great success. / We took more orders than ever before and the visits / after the conference were extremely promising. At the closing ceremony, / Dr Strong, the conference president, made some very kind remarks / about our company's stand. Our team did a first-class / job and they are to be congratulated.

During the conference / I took the opportunity to assess the competition. The number / of firms attending has greatly increased and next year there / will be even more firms wishing to take part. New / products were to be seen everywhere and were a reminder / of the strength of our competitors.

I chaired a meeting / of the sales team and expressed my thanks for their / efforts. I attended one of the training programmes for junior / sales representatives; these courses are playing a major part in / our recent success in this market. Although costly and somewhat / difficult to administrate, I think it is by far the / best investment we have made in this area.

The next / conference is in Zimbabwe. I strongly recommend we take part. / **(180 words)**

## SPEED DEVELOPMENT

Turn to page 40 and the letter which begins, *'Dear Sir, I am writing to confirm . . .'*.

This letter contains 100 words. Many of the outlines are theory examples, short forms and phrases reviewed in this unit.

### Your aim

To take this letter at a speed at least 20 wam above your average.

### Your action

1  Read through the shorthand and identify outlines which cause hesitancy.
2  Drill those outlines until there is no hesitation.
3  Repeat the reading until you can call it rapid reading.
4  Copy the letter into your notebook, writing quickly and, at the same time, writing accurately.
5  Rapid read the printed shorthand one more time. The material is now totally familiar to you, and you know and can write each outline without any hesitancy.
6  Take the letter from dictation at 20 wam above your average speed. Check outlines. Repeat dictation. Check outlines and repeat dictation.

# UNIT 5
## Halving

In words of one syllable light strokes are halved for **T** and darker strokes for **D**:

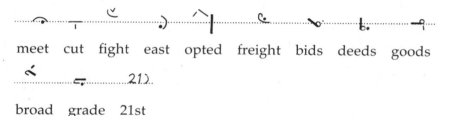

meet   cut   fight   east   opted   freight   bids   deeds   goods

broad   grade   21st

In words of more than one syllable, and when a stroke has a final hook or a final joined diphthong, strokes are halved for **T** or **D**:

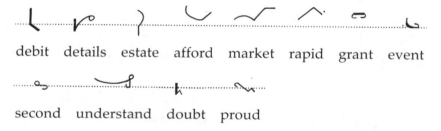

debit   details   estate   afford   market   rapid   grant   event

second   understand   doubt   proud

Strokes **M** and **N** are halved and thickened to indicate a following **D**:

moderation   medical   indication   send   sound   standard   22nd

## The halving principle is *not* used:

When a half-length stroke with a joined diphthong, eg
**doubt**, is followed by the sound of **S**; or when the halving would
not show clearly:

doubts   droughts   feuds   allocate   factory   select   vacate

When a vowel follows final **T** or **D**, as there must be a full stroke
to be able to place the vowel sign:

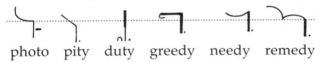

photo   pity   duty   greedy   needy   remedy

When **upward R** stands alone, to avoid confusion with certain
short forms; or when a vowel comes between **L–D** and
**R–D**:

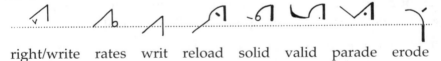

right/write   rates   writ   reload   solid   valid   parade   erode

## Disjoined strokes

For the sake of legibility a half-length **T** or **D** immediately
following stroke **T** or **D** is disjoined:

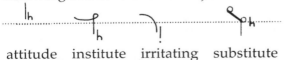

attitude   institute   irritating   substitute

## Theory revision drill

### A circular letter   *HOMEWORK.*

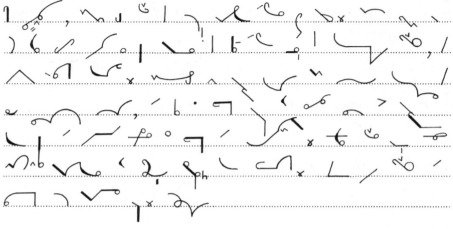

## Key

Dear Householder, I hope you do not find it irritating / to receive offers through the post. I am proud to / say this one really is different because it does offer / goods at factory prices, which represent solid value. I understand / how people feel about many firms which send similar mail, / and it is a great pity that as a result / some of the public have doubts and regard such companies / as greedy and unreliable. This company fights to cut costs / and also believes that there is no substitute for quality. / Check our prices and select your bargains today. Yours sincerely /

**(100 words)**

## Short Forms

cannot    could    gentleman    gentlemen    immediate    immediately

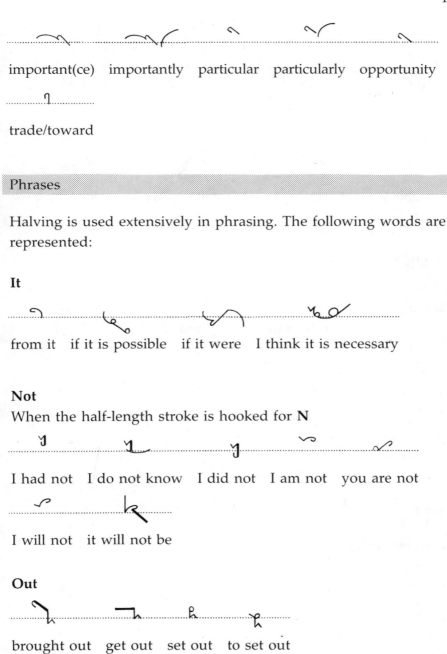

important(ce)   importantly   particular   particularly   opportunity

trade/toward

## Phrases

Halving is used extensively in phrasing. The following words are represented:

**It**

from it    if it is possible    if it were    I think it is necessary

**Not**

When the half-length stroke is hooked for **N**

I had not    I do not know    I did not    I am not    you are not

I will not    it will not be

**Out**

brought out    get out    set out    to set out

50

## Time

some time   at some time   at the same time   from time to time

## To

I am able to   we are able to   you will be able to   able to make

I am unable to   in order to

## Would

Represented by the short form ...₂...... and also by half-length ...✓....

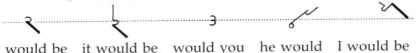

would be   it would be   would you   he would   I would be

this would   if it would

Intersection

**Th** ...( ... **month**

Short form and theory drill

**Memo**                    HomEWORK.

**To: Branch Managers   From: General Manager**

**Subject: Staff meetings**

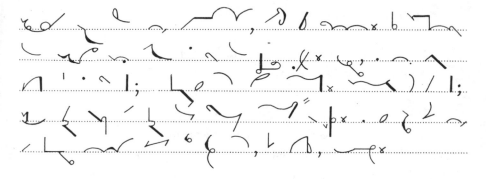

**Key**

I think it is necessary to have staff meetings regularly, / rather than just from time to time. It is of / great importance for individuals to meet and have an opportunity / for discussions each month. If it is possible, the meeting / should be held on a particular day; it could be / the first or last Monday. I am unable to say / which day; I do not know which would be better / and it would be for the branch manager to decide. / The first of these short meetings should take place immediately / – that is this month or, at the latest, next month. /                    **(100 words)**

## SKILL DEVELOPMENT

### Half-length strokes

*Exaggerate* the size of each half-length stroke by making it less than half-length.

When transcribing your shorthand notes there must never be any doubt in your mind about the size of strokes. Aim for consistency. Ordinary strokes are always the same size; half-length strokes are less than half; and double-length strokes are more than double.

If necessary, change your writing style, but always write each stroke so that it is instantly recognisable.

## CORRESPONDENCE

Two letters and a staff notice concerning the Select Clothing Company Limited.

### Letter to: Chief Buyer, National Stores Limited

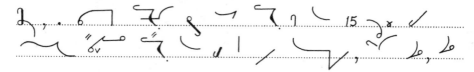

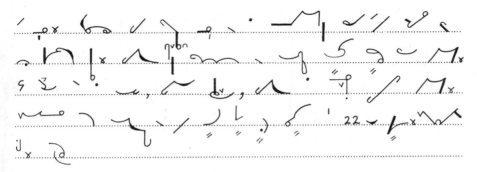

## Key

Dear Sir, The Select Clothing Company Limited has been in / the clothing trade for 15 years. We manufacture high-class / clothing for gentlemen at our factory, particularly shirts, shorts and / coats. This means we produce goods to a guaranteed standard / and are always able to meet delivery dates. We have / tried from time to time to interest National Stores in / our range. With the appointment of a new, young designer, / we have an exciting winter range. I enclose your invitation / to our Show at The East Hotel on 22nd / July. I hope you are able to attend. Yours faithfully / **(100 words)**

## Letter to Mrs J Robinson, Fashion Market Fabrics Limited

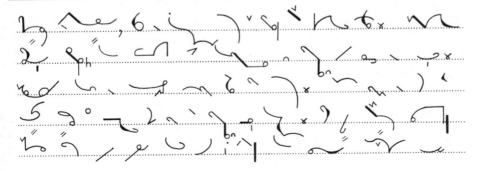

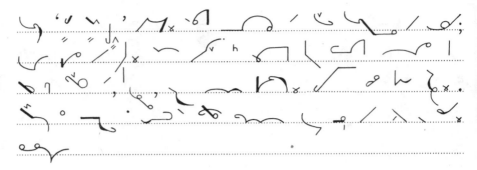

## Key

Dear Mrs Robinson, This is to confirm the order I / placed by telephone this morning. I believe there is no / substitute for quality and the fabrics you produce are second / to none. I think it is necessary for you to / understand the importance of this particular order. I am proud / to say that National Stores has given us the opportunity / of producing goods for them. Their Chief Buyer selected items / from our recent fashion show but opted for something entirely / new for their 'Gentleman About Town' range. Solid colours and / fine fabrics are necessary; full details are attached. I am / relying on you to select top quality materials at best / trade prices and, if it is possible, to have immediate / delivery. Work starts at the end of this month. The / buyer has given an indication of more business from time / to time if the goods are up to standard. Sincerely /          **(150 words)**

## Staff notice about overtime

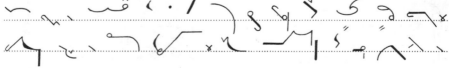

## Key

I am proud to announce that a large order has / been placed by the National Stores group. We have had / to fight to secure this work. I have guaranteed that / the goods will be up to standard and that the / delivery date will be met. In order to do this / it will be necessary to organise an overtime shift from / 22nd July to the end of August. The hours / will be 1800 to 2100, at the / usual overtime rates. For those staying on duty after the / normal 1730 hours finish, refreshments will be provided in / the factory canteen, free of charge. A minibus will be / available to take staff home each evening.

Because of individual / summer holiday commitments I quite understand that some staff will / have a valid reason for opting out. However, I think / it is necessary to stress the importance of this work. / In this very competitive market we cannot afford to fail. / With co-operation, and the right attitude, I know we will / be able to make a success of this particular job. /     **(180 words)**

## SPEED DEVELOPMENT

Turn to page 51 and the passage which begins, *'I think it is necessary . . .'*.

This letter contains many of the short forms, phrases and intersections reviewed in this unit.

### Your aim

To master short forms and phrases and to be able to write these outlines rapidly to increase your writing speed.

### Your action

1   Read the passage as quickly as you can. Time yourself. There are only 100 words and it should take you less than a minute. Make a note of any outlines which you cannot read, or which cause you to hesitate.
2   Drill those outlines.
3   Repeat steps 1 and 2 until you can read the passage very quickly and without any hesitation.
4   Take the passage from dictation, by having someone read to you or by recording it yourself on a tape.
5   Repeat the dictation several times but always read through the printed shorthand as quickly as you can before taking the next dictation.

# UNIT 6
## Strokes N and NG; N hook

The two forms of representing **N**, the stroke and the hook, are reviewed in this unit. Once again, it is mainly a matter of vowel indication. The presence or absence of an initial vowel, or a final vowel, determines which form of **N** is used.

Having indicated the vowels in this way, it is usually unnecessary to insert them in the outline. Remember, vowels are always placed to strokes: you cannot place a vowel to a hook.

### Stroke N

**Stroke N** is used:

When **N**–vowel/diphthong or circle **S** plus **N** ends a word

avenue    revenue    county    deny    many    money    now    listen

When a vowel/diphthong occurs between **N** and **S/Z**, to enable the vowel to be placed

bonus    illness    minus    modernise    sickness    venues

To represent the light sound of **NS** and **NSES**

allowance    announces    balance    circumstances    convenience

finance    offences

In the middle of an outline (the exceptions to this are given in the
**N hook** section)

arrange   coincide   council   electronic   extensive   residential

## Stroke NG

bank    amongst    angry    longer    stronger

**Note:** *any longer    no longer,*

## N hook

Remember, the hook is added to the *end* of a stroke, inside
curves, eg  **phone**, and clockwise to straight strokes,
eg **open**.

The **N hook** is used as follows:

When the sound of **N** ends a word

alone   telephone   union   again   between   certain   return

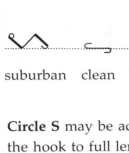

suburban   clean

**Circle S** may be added to **N hook** by writing a tiny circle inside the hook to full length *curved* strokes to give the sound of **NZ**. When added to half-length strokes, **circle S** represents **S** *or* **Z**:

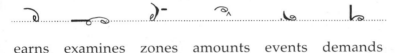

earns   examines   zones   amounts   events   demands

**Circle S**, representing the sound **S** or **Z**, is added to **N hook** to *straight* strokes by closing the hook; **SES circle** and the **ST loop** are added in the same way:

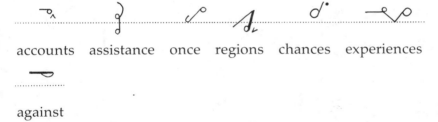

accounts   assistance   once   regions   chances   experiences

against

When a root word ends with **N hook** it is retained in derivatives; otherwise **N hook** is not used in the middle of an outline:

certainly   appointment   morning   landlord   *but*   guaranteed

branches

## -MENT

This word ending is represented by half-length **M** hooked for **N** ⌒, but when it is not easy or possible to make this joining, use half-length **stroke N** .⌄.

arrangement   management   settlement   achievement

department   government

## Theory revision drill

### Letter from the City Council Planning Office   *HomeWoRk.*

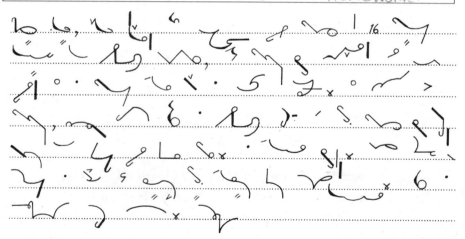

### Key

Dear Mr Evans, I have been advised that you no / longer use the premises at 16 Branch Avenue for residential / purposes, and that the property has been modernised and is / now used as a branch

office by a national insurance / company. As landlord of the
property you must be aware / that this is a residential zone and
planning permission has / to be obtained before any change of
use takes place. / An offence has been committed. I must ask you
to / arrange an appointment with the Senior Planning Officer at
your / earliest convenience. This is an extremely urgent matter.
Yours truly /                                          **(100 words)**

## Short forms

any/in   anybody   anyhow   anyone   anything   anyway

enlarge   enlargement   enlarger   financial(ly)   general(ly)

inconvenience/ inconvenient(ly)   indifferent   influence   insurance

January   opinion

## Phrases

The **N hook** is used in phrasing to represent three very
frequently-occurring words:

**Been**

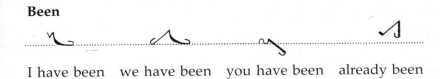

I have been   we have been   you have been   already been

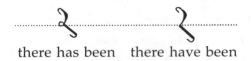

there has been    there have been

**Own**

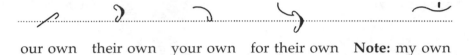

our own   their own   your own   for their own   **Note:** my own

**Than**

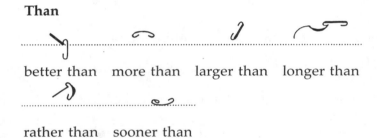

better than   more than   larger than   longer than

rather than   sooner than

**Once, next**

These are abbreviated in phrases:

at once   once again   next month   next week

Intersection

N  **enquire/inquire**
     **enquiry/inquiry**

## Short form and phrasing drill

### Letter to the Claims Department, Countrywide Insurance Company Limited

## Key

Dear Sir, Our January stocktaking revealed we are minus one / electronic typewriter, and I am of the opinion that it / has been stolen. I am unaware of anyone other than / staff having access. Extensive inquiries have been made without success. / I now wish to claim on our current insurance policy. / I telephoned the police at once and an officer has / already been to take details. Rather than wait for a / claim form, I have obtained an estimate for a replacement / machine. The loss is inconvenient and in the circumstances I / trust that an early settlement will be possible. Yours faithfully / **(100 words)**

## SKILL DEVELOPMENT

**F/V and N hooks**   If you ever confuse these hooks, refer back to Unit 4 and carry out the steps set out on page 39.

**Punctuation**   When you hear punctuation given, as in most examinations, and sometimes in the office, or when you recognise the need for a punctuation sign, always write it immediately.

The following are the most important punctuation signs:

*A full stop sign* (written as a single stroke ✗ ) completely removes the problem of running sentences together. In your notes you must write all full stops marking the ends of sentences.

*Two upward dashes* ( ....... ) under an outline to indicate a proper noun (name) make transcription so much easier.

*A new paragraph sign* ( .../..... ) should always be written, either during dictation or added when editing your notes. Marks may be lost in examinations if paragraphs are not shown in the transcript. Omission of paragraphs in the office would make a piece of work unacceptable.

## CORRESPONDENCE

A letter, memo and press release concerning the County Building Company Limited.

---

### Letter to the Chief Planning Officer

---

### Key

Dear Sir, I am seeking permission for a new surburban /
shopping development in the northern zone of the city, and /
attach an outline plan. I have been guaranteed full financial /
backing by our bank. The site which the company owns / is
much larger than required and the balance of the / land beyond
the development, marked green on the plan, will / be for houses.
It is intended to invest a large / sum of money and meet demand
in this region for / residences. Work on the shops should begin
sooner than the / application shows and your assistance would
be appreciated. Yours faithfully /                    **(100 words)**

Memo
To: Site Manager   From: General Manager
Subject: County Shopping Plaza

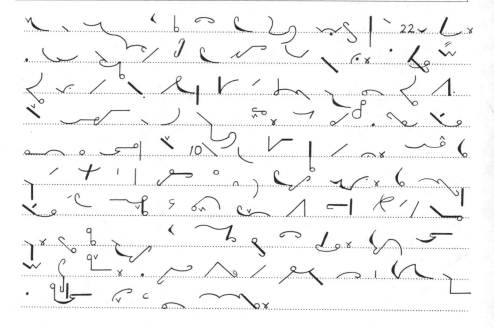

Key

I have to inform you that it is more than / ever essential to meet
the completion date of 22nd / January. The financial penalties are
larger than ever and we / cannot afford to be late. A large
number of inquiries / about the shops to let are being received
daily and / it is important to have some shops ready by next /
week to show potential clients. In the circumstances the present /
bonus scheme is increased by 10 per cent if target / dates are
met. Announce this today and enlarge on it / once again as you
see everyone individually. This improved bonus / offer coincides

with the higher overtime rate agreed last month / and which begins today. Please stress to everyone that management / has been more than generous. They were angry about the / threatened strike. The union representatives are reasonable men but they / will have to take a stronger line with some members. /

**(150 words)**

---

**Press release for the *Daily News***

68

## Key

The County Building Company is pleased to announce the opening / of the County Shopping Plaza just off North Avenue / on 22nd January. This venture has been given full / Government support and the approval of the City Council. The / Mayor will perform the opening ceremony at 11 am / and members of the public are invited to attend.

Branches / of many national stores are amongst the first shops to / open, together with a number of local firms which have / moved out of the city centre. One shop is still / vacant and available for rental. There are a number of / residential properties within the plaza area for sale. This is / the first announcement to the public about these one and / two-bedroom apartments. They have all the convenience of suburban / living, with excellent public transport and the added bonus of / superb shopping facilities. There is a range of prices, determined / by the size and location; the most expensive have two / bedrooms, their own verandah and fine views over the plaza / gardens; all represent excellent value. Viewing is by appointment only. /      **(180 words)**

## SPEED DEVELOPMENT

Turn to page 65 and the passage which begins, *'Dear Sir, I am seeking . . .'*.
This passage contains 100 words.

### Your aim

To be able to read and write each outline without hesitation.

### Your action

1   Read through the letter and circle with a pencil any outline which causes you to hesitate.
2   Check each encircled outline with the key.
3   Drill these outlines (refer to page vi to see what drilling really means).
4   Re-read the letter several times until you can read through it completely without any hesitation. This is the test. When you can do this it means you do know the outlines.
5   Take the letter from dictation. Which outlines caused you to hesitate when taking the dictation? Identify these by re-reading the printed shorthand and then drill these outlines. Repeat the dictation at least three times.

# UNIT 7
## Doubling

Strokes may be doubled in length to indicate the additional sound of **TER, DER, THR** or **TURE**.

## Curved strokes

These are doubled as follows:

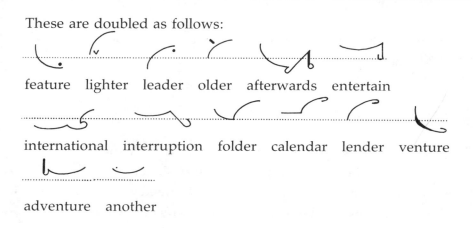

feature   lighter   leader   older   afterwards   entertain

international   interruption   folder   calendar   lender   venture

adventure   another

## Straight strokes

Straight strokes are doubled *only* when following another stroke or having a final hook:

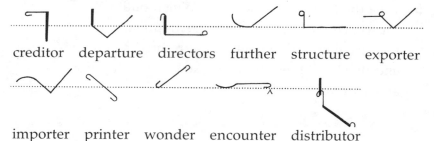

creditor   departure   directors   further   structure   exporter

importer   printer   wonder   encounter   distributor

**Circular letter to customers**   HOMEWORK

*[shorthand outlines]*

**Key**

Dear Customer, As Managing Director of Finer Furniture Limited, I / am pleased to announce details of our forthcoming winter sale. / Please make a note in your diary or on your / calendar that 5 January is the opening date of our / Winter Wonder Sale. A special feature this year will be / furniture from international as well as leading national manufacturers. The / sale will continue without interruption throughout January. After 31 / January the price of each item of furniture will be / increased by a further 10 per cent; this is due / to the recent price rise set by manufacturers. Yours sincerely / **(100 words)**

72

## Short forms

character   characteristic   wonderful/ly   therefore   manufacture

manufacturer   maximum   minimum   misrepresent   their/there

## Phrases

**Their/there, other**

A stroke may be doubled in length for the addition of **their, there** or **other**:

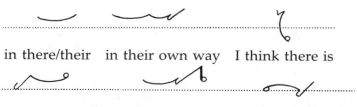

in there/their   in their own way   I think there is

we know there is   in other words   some other way

**Order**

**Stroke N** hooked for **R** is doubled for the addition of **order**:

in order   in order that

## Intersection

**M** ⌒ **morning**

HOMEWORK

## Short form and phrasing drill

### Letter to a customer from Office Furniture Manufacturing Co Ltd

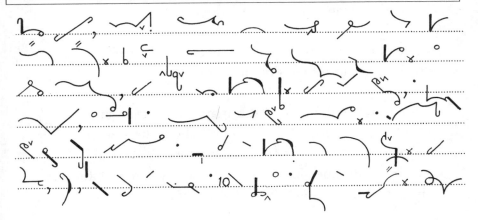

### Key

Dear Miss Winter, I am writing in order that you / may
understand the reason for the delay in your order. / It is quite out
of character for this firm to / have delays. As responsible
manufacturers, we strive to meet delivery / dates. One of our
suppliers, a timber importer, has caused / an interruption in the
supply of materials. An alternative supply / has been obtained
and we know there is a good / chance of delivering your order on
Friday morning. We ask / you, therefore, to be patient and to
accept a 10 / per cent discount as a gesture of goodwill.
Yours sincerely / **(100 words)**

## SKILL DEVELOPMENT

### Doubling

Because it is so important, advice similar to that given in Unit 5, Halving, is repeated here.

*Exaggerate* the size of each double-length stroke by making it more than double length.

When transcribing your shorthand notes there must never be any doubt in your mind about the size of strokes. Aim for consistency. Ordinary strokes are always the same size; half-length strokes are less than half; and double-length strokes are more than double.

If necessary, change your writing style but always write each stroke so that it is instantly recognisable.

## CORRESPONDENCE

Two letters and a memo from International Builders and Engineers Limited.

## Letter to the Manager, International Recruitment Agency

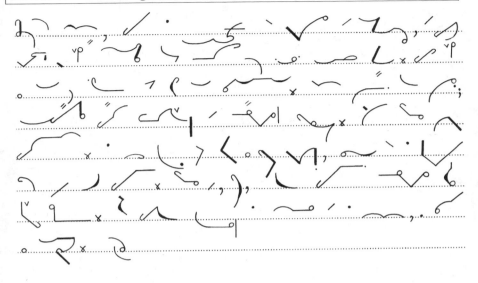

## Key

Dear Sir or Madam, We are an international company of /
builders and engineers, and wish to recruit two site managers /
for the calendar year commencing next January. One site is / in
East Africa and the other in Hong Kong. I / am looking for
leaders, in other words well qualified and / experienced
personnel. Older applicants will be welcome. A main feature / of
each job is bridge building, something of a departure / from our
usual work. Applicants should, therefore, have working
experience / on this type of structure. Although we have fixed a /
maximum and a minimum, the salary is negotiable. Yours
faithfully /                                              **(100 words)**

76

## Letter to Mr G Mitchell from the Personnel Manager

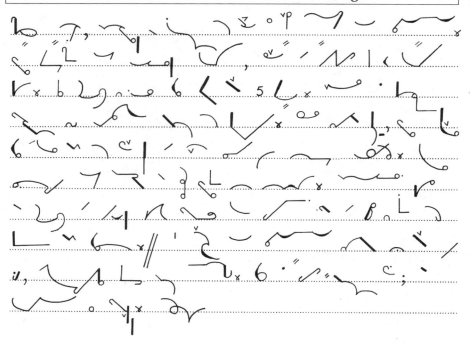

## Key

Dear Mr Mitchell, I am pleased to confirm your appointment / as Site Manager in Hong Kong. Please check the contract / in the enclosed folder, sign and return it without further / delay. It is essential you commence this job by 5 / January. I know there is a domestic problem you have / to resolve before your departure. As soon as you are / able to do so, please advise this office about your / flight date and my secretary will make the necessary arrangements. / If there is some other way in which I can / be of assistance, please contact me immediately. I am enclosing / details of essential and recommended health precautions for working abroad / and suggest you contact your own doctor about this matter. /

On arrival in Hong Kong you will be met by / our agent, and afterwards taken to your accommodation. This is / a one-bedroom flat; all furniture is provided. Yours sincerely /

**(150 words)**

| Memo |
| To: **Site Managers, Nairobi and Hong Kong** |
| From: **General Manager** |
| Subject: **Visit in April** |

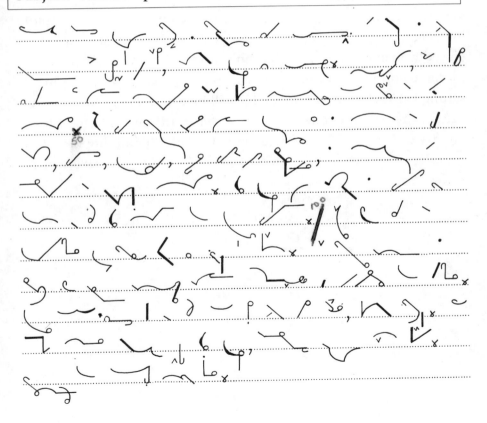

| Key |
|-----|

In order that I can fully appreciate the problems you / are encountering and obtain an up-to-date picture / of the situation at each site, I will be visiting / you next month. Meanwhile, I would suggest you check with / local importers about the delays and interruptions in supplies of / raw materials. Although we prefer to use local firms as / a matter of general policy, we can, if necessary, use / one of our own subsidiary companies, a manufacturer and exporter / of building materials. This visit will also be a wonderful / opportunity for me to assess this market for future work. /

    I think there is every chance of further contracts if / the present job is completed on time. I propose to / make a special effort to speak to managers of local / organisations who are responsible for large contracts. If there is / anything you can do to assist in setting up such / appointments, it will be appreciated. In order to get the / maximum benefit out of this visit, I expect you to / fill my diary. Please make arrangements for entertaining important contacts. / **(180 words)**

## SPEED DEVELOPMENT

Turn to page 71 and the passage which begins, *'Dear Customer . . .'*. This letter contains many examples of the theory being reviewed in this unit. Some of the outlines will be new to you. Spend as much time as it takes you to learn the new outlines.

### Your aim

To master new outlines through rapid reading.

### Your action

First of all, turn to page vi *'How to use this book'* and read paragraph 3. Follow these instructions whenever rapid reading is mentioned.

1  Rapid read the letter, checking the key if necessary.
2  Repeat this reading until all points of hesitancy have been overcome.
3  Take the letter from dictation at least 3 times. Make the most of a cassette player if you have one, or persuade someone to dictate to you by reading from the key. In between each dictation, rapid read the printed shorthand.

# UNIT 8
## Stroke L; L hook

The sound of **L** is represented by a stroke (upward or downward) and also by a hook.

## Stroke L

When **L**, or **vowel plus L**, begins a word, or **L plus vowel** ends a word, the stroke is used; the stroke **L** is also used in the middle of an outline.

**Stroke L** is written upwards, except after **N** ⌒ and **NG** ⌒ when it is written downwards to allow an easier joining:

allow   alone   elect   excellent   leading   learn   believe   belong

annual   manual   personal   personnel   until   amazingly

willingly

The suffix **-LY** is represented by stroke **L**, joined or disjoined:

cheaply   exceedingly   hardly   quarterly   recently   rightly

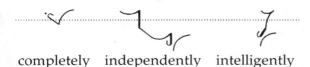

completely   independently   intelligently

The hook is used when the sound of **L** is combined with another consonant and there is no vowel in between.

### L hook to straight strokes
This small hook is written at the beginning of a straight stroke, on the same side as circle S. Write the hook first. It may also be written in the middle of an outline. **Circle S** is written inside the hook; write the tiny circle first and then form the hook:

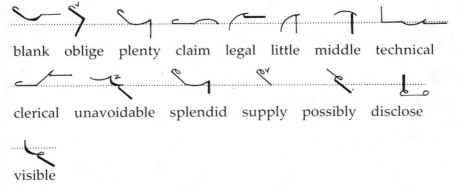

blank   oblige   plenty   claim   legal   little   middle   technical

clerical   unavoidable   splendid   supply   possibly   disclose

visible

### L hook to curved strokes
A large hook at the beginning of curved strokes, inside the curve, adds **L**. Write the hook first. The hook may also be used in the middle of an outline; **circle S** is written inside the hook:

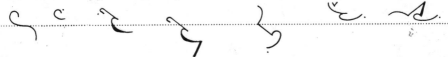

floor   flat   approval   privilege   especially   finally   marginally

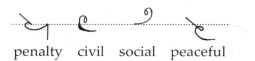

penalty   civil   social   peaceful

**FL** 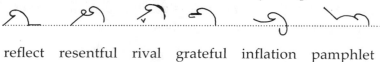 and **VL** are always reversed after an upstroke or a horizontal stroke, to allow an easier joining:

reflect   resentful   rival   grateful   inflation   pamphlet

The **FL/VL hook** is used in derivatives of words ending with the **F/V hook**:

objective   objectively   brief   briefly   effective   effectively

Theory revision drill

Extract from a report to shareholders   HOMEWORK.

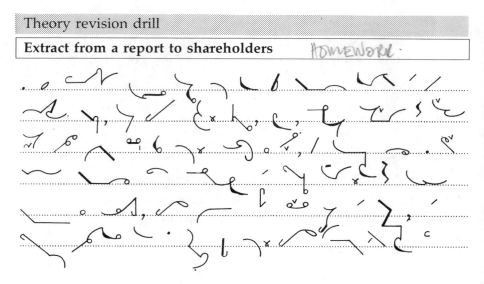

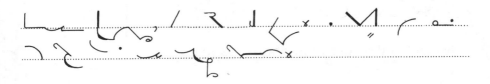

## Key

The first quarterly figures for this year have just become /
available and are marginally better, for which we are thankful. /
It appears, however, exceedingly unlikely that the final annual
results / will be as good as this year. Inflation is rising, / which
effectively means the supply of money becomes more expensive /
and profits fall. Although the financial picture is uncertain, we /
must look at all the signs intelligently and objectively, and /
prepare ourselves for an especially difficult year. We must keep /
up with technical developments, which cannot be done cheaply.
The / Board will seek your approval for a new investment
programme. /                                              **(100 words)**

## Short forms

| are | influential | thank | thankful | that | will | year | your |
|-----|-------------|-------|----------|------|------|------|------|

yourself   responsible/responsibility

## Phrases

**Stroke L** is very useful in phrases as follows:

it will be    you will have    will you    as early as possible

this letter

**L hook** adds the word **all** to strokes **T** and **B**, and **only** to stroke **N**:

**All**

at all    at all times    by all    by all means    by all accounts

**Only**

it is only    if only    it will only be

## Intersection

**Downward R**  arrange/arranged/arrangement
arranging

Memo

To: Factory Manager   From: Managing Director

Subject: Delivery dates

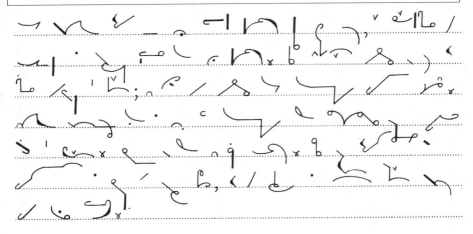

Key

In the belief that we could meet agreed delivery dates /
throughout the year, I signed contracts which included a
penalty / clause for late delivery. It is my responsibility to see /
that contracts are completed on time; you alone are responsible /
for the factory work schedules. You will have to make /
arrangements for a meeting with factory staff as early as /
possible to discuss the union ban on overtime. Speak to / staff
you consider influential. Stress to them that we will / all welcome
a speedy and peaceful settlement, without which it / is only a
matter of time before we face closure. /          **(100 words)**

## SKILL DEVELOPMENT

**L Hook and R Hook**   Confusion between these two hooks must be avoided. Accurate notes are essential for accurate transcription.

Refer back to Unit 4, page 39, for advice.

**The** is represented by the short form and also by the tick. Use the tick whenever possible, because it is quicker to write and avoids confusion between the short form **the** and the short form **a/an**.

The tick cannot be used at the beginning of a sentence, or after the **ST** or **STR loop**, **NS** or **NSES** circle, or a **half-length stroke** standing alone.

To avoid confusion, always write **the** exactly on the line and **a/an** well above the line. More marks are lost in shorthand examinations because of confusion over these two short forms than any other error.

## CORRESPONDENCE

Three letters to and from British World Airways.

## A letter of complaint from Miss J Little to the Manager, British World Airways

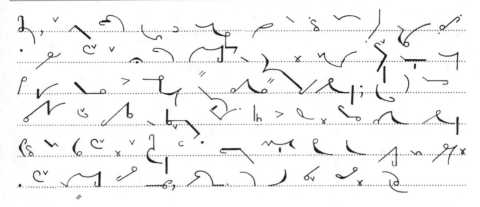

## Key

Dear Sir, I should be grateful if you would investigate / the list of complaints I am attaching to this letter / concerning a recent flight I made from London to Zimbabwe. / I feel obliged to go into such detail because of / the exceedingly poor service received; even so I can hardly / find words to describe the appalling attitude of the staff. / By all accounts you will have received other complaints about / this flight. I travelled with a group and I know / that several have written to you recently. The flight to / London was excellent, reflecting your usual high standards. Yours faithfully / **(100 words)**

## Letter to Miss J Little from the Customer Services Manager

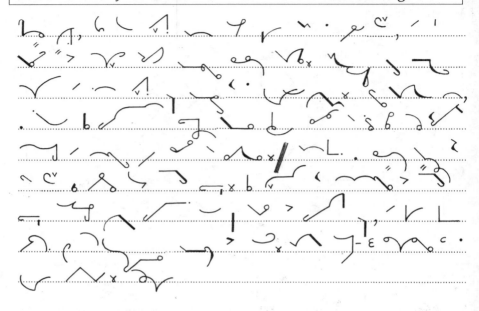

## Key

Dear Miss Little, Thank you for writing to me in / such detail about a recent flight, and on behalf of / the airline I wish to express sincere apologies. I have / only just been given your letter and am writing today / to explain that a full inquiry will be made. Please / believe me, the company does welcome criticism because it is / only as a result of complaints such as yours that / we are able to maintain and improve our standards of / service.

I am contacting the Senior Purser of that particular / flight, who is responsible for the cabin crew. It is / likely that members of the cabin crew in question will / be working in different parts of the world today, and / it will take roughly three or four weeks to gather / all the information. I will be in touch with you / as early as possible with a full report. Yours sincerely / **(150 words)**

89

## Circular letter to travel agent managers

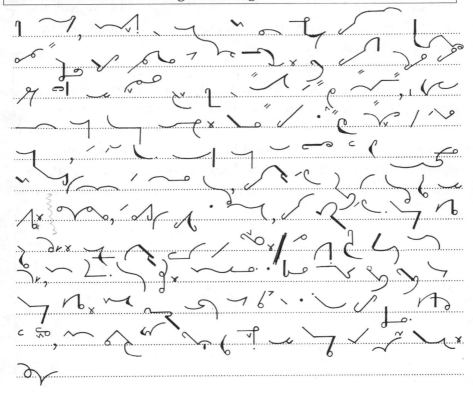

## Key

Dear Manager, I am writing to inform you about some /
exceedingly welcome developments as a result of discussions
between ourselves / and the Government. British World Airways
was recently granted new / licences to fly direct to North and
South America, but / they will only come into effect next month.
Because we / are a civil airline which operates independently,
and not having / entered into any agreements with other
international companies about minimum / and maximum fares,

we will be able to offer especially / low fares on these new routes. As early as possible, / and certainly within a month, we will also be offering / package holidays to these areas. No other company will be / able to equal our prices.

As the leading travel agency / in your area, I am asking for your assistance. I / am enclosing an advance copy of the special brochure for / the package holidays. I know that you can be influential / in the choice of a company when discussing holiday arrangements / with clients, and I am hopeful that you will promote / these exciting new packages to our mutual benefit. Yours sincerely / **(180 words)**

## SPEED DEVELOPMENT

Turn to page 87 and the passage which begins, *'Dear Sir, I should be grateful . . .'*.

    This letter contains 100 words. Many of the outlines are theory examples, short forms and phrases reviewed in this unit.

### Your aim

To take this letter at a speed at least 20 wam above your average.

### Your action

1  Read through the shorthand and identify outlines which cause hesitancy.
2  Drill those outlines until any hesitation is removed.
3  Repeat the reading until you can call it rapid reading.
4  Copy the letter into your notebook, writing quickly and, at the same time, writing accurately.
5  Rapid read the printed shorthand one more time. The material is now totally familiar to you. You now know and can write each outline without any hesitancy.
6  Take the letter from dictation at 20 wam above your average speed. Check outlines. Repeat dictation. Check outlines and repeat dictation.

# UNIT 9
## H

There are two forms of **H**, a stroke and a tick.

## Stroke H

**Stroke H** is written upwards

handles   heading   height   heat   hence   hesitate   hotel   higher

highest   highlights   hurry   whose

When **H** comes in the middle of an outline, begin the stroke by writing it like a circle S, anti-clockwise, and as the circle is completed take the stroke straight up,

eg **perhaps**

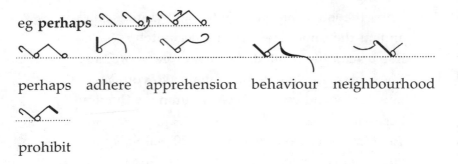

perhaps   adhere   apprehension   behaviour   neighbourhood

prohibit

When **H** follows a curved stroke, the circle which forms the beginning of **stroke H** is written on the *outside* of the curve

enhance   inhabit   unhappy   likelihood   shareholder

When **S** occurs in the middle of a word immediately followed by **H**, omit the **H**

householder   leasehold   mishap

## Tick H

HOMLIER

**Tick H**, written downwards, is used before **M, upward L** and **downward R**

him   human   helpful   health   holiday   harmful   harmony

**Note:** Contrast the angle of short form **to** ⟍ with **tick H** ⟋

## Theory revision drill

| Circular letter from a Health Centre | HOMEWORK. |

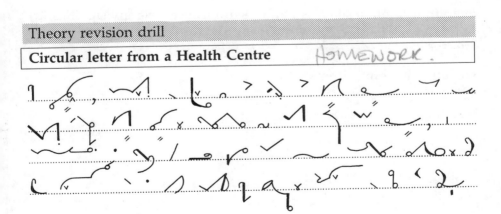

94

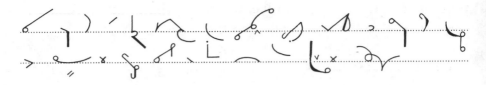

## Key

Dear Householder, I am writing to advise you of the / opening of the Health Centre in the new building opposite / the Holiday Hotel. Perhaps you have already heard about the / Centre, but I am enclosing a brochure which gives details / of our many neighbourhood services. There is every likelihood of / a rush to register during the first few days. I / would like to stress that there is no hurry to / do so and it would be helpful if householders wishing / to register would spread their visits to the Centre. Please / do not hesitate to contact me for advice. Yours sincerely / **(100 words)**

## Short forms

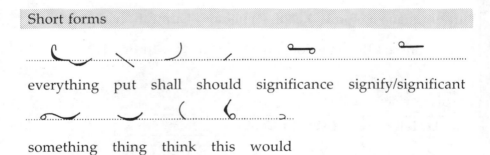

everything   put   shall   should   significance   signify/significant

something   thing   think   this   would

## Phrases

### He

At the beginning of a phrase, or standing alone, the outline is written in full

he is   he will be

In the middle or at the end of a phrase ...ı... is used:

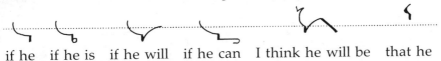

if he   if he is   if he will   if he can   I think he will be   that he

**Note:** This abbreviated outline cannot stand alone.

### Hope

I hope that   I hope you will   I hope you are   we hope that

we hope you will

## Intersection

**KR** ⌐‾‾ **corporation**

## Short form and phrasing drill

### Letter to the Secretary, Chamber of Commerce HOMEWORK.

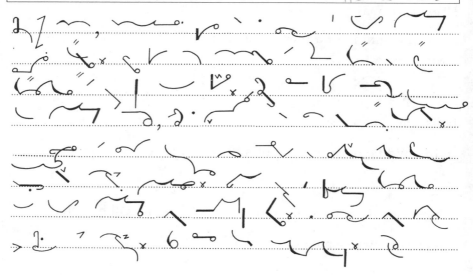

## Key

Dear Sir/Madam, I am enclosing details of a seminar / on Foreign Language Skills for Business. Please tell your members / and ask them to free themselves and put the date / in their diaries. There has been significant additional Government finance / for language courses, and there is a likelihood of more / becoming available. International corporations and small firms must export to / survive and have everything to gain by employing linguists. Young / people who distinguish themselves in foreign languages should be guaranteed / jobs. The seminar should be helpful to the trainer and / the employer. This has significance for all involved. Yours faithfully /

**(100 words)**

## SKILL DEVELOPMENT

### Notebook use

1 Use a notebook with a spiral binding to allow pages to lie flat and give a good writing surface.

2 Open the book fully and work through page by page, using and filling each line.

3 Rule up a margin on several pages in advance of taking dictation. Use the margin to add query signs about points you wish to check with the dictator, and to insert corrected outlines; do not alter outlines within the notes.

4 Date the first page of each session of dictation by writing it at the foot of the page.

5 Keep hold of a bottom corner of the page with finger and thumb of the non-writing hand. As the bottom of the page is reached, quickly turn the page; continue writing on the next page and, without looking, feel your way down the page and once again take hold of the corner.

## CORRESPONDENCE

A letter, memo and draft of a brochure from the Managing Director, International Hotel Corporation.

## Letter to Mr J Hill, Director, Harmony Record Company

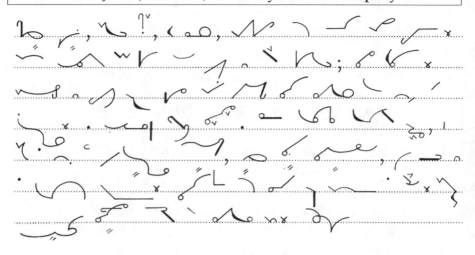

## Key

Dear Mr Hill, I have been trying, without success, to / return your call of last week. I am unhappy about / the delay in reaching you by telephone; hence this letter. / I understand you wish to have details of our range / of hotel services for meetings and conferences. The enclosed brochure / highlights the significant facilities available to clients, but I think / a meeting with our Conference Manager, Mr Harry Henderson, will / give you a fuller picture. He will contact your secretary / today to make an appointment. I hope that the International / Hotels Corporation can be of service to you. Yours sincerely / **(100 words)**

**Memo**
**To: Conference Manager    From: Managing Director**
**Subject: Client visits**

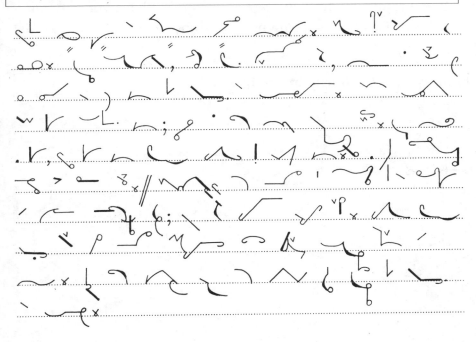

**Key**

Please contact Mr Hill of Harmony Records immediately. I have /
been trying all week without success. If he is unavailable, / and
there is every likelihood of that, make an appointment / through
his secretary to see him at the beginning of / next week. I am
unhappy about the delay in contacting / him; he is a very
important potential business client. If / he mentions the delay,
please tell him everything we have / been doing to reach him.
The attached correspondence explains all / the significant points.

I hope you will be able to / complete your calls on managers of

100

central and local government / departments this month; put all
other work to one side. / We have everything to gain by such
calls and I / think we can more than justify the investment of
time / and money. It would be very helpful to have your / report
on these visits at the beginning of next month. /     **(150 words)**

**Draft of new publicity brochure**

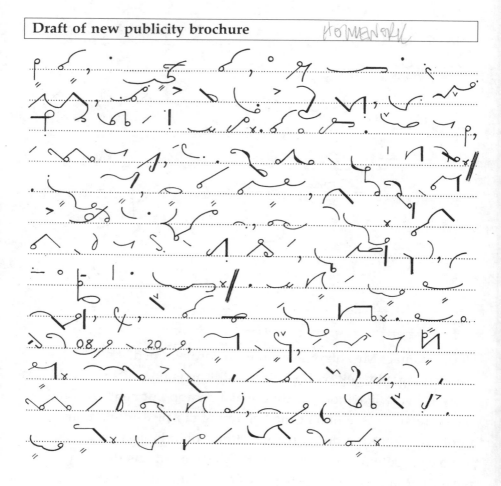

## Key

City Hotel, an International Corporation hotel, has recently undergone a / complete refurbishment, enhancing all the best features of the original / building, fully modernising existing facilities and adding new ones. The / hotel is once again the finest in the city, and / perhaps in the region, offering the very best service to / visitors on holiday or business.

The Conference Manager, Mr Harry / Henderson, will be very pleased to handle all the necessary / arrangements for a shareholders' meeting, seminar or conference. He will / be happy to assist in the planning of wedding receptions / and, if he is requested to do so, will act / as toastmaster at a function.

The new Health and Fitness / Centre may be used, free of charge, by hotel guests / and conference delegates. The Centre is open from 08 / 00 hours to 2000 hours, Monday to Friday, and / mornings only on Saturday and Sunday. Members of the public / who are unhappy about their weight, or who perhaps are / just simply health conscious, may use these facilities by joining / the Fitness Club. Full details are available from the Secretary. /

**(180 words)**

## SPEED DEVELOPMENT

Turn to page 96 and the passage which begins 'Dear Sir/Madam, . . .'.

This letter contains many of the short forms, phrases and intersections reviewed in this unit.

### Your aim

To master short forms and phrases and to be able to write these outlines rapidly to increase your writing speed.

### Your action

1   Read the passage as quickly as you can. Time yourself. There are only 100 words and it should take you less than a minute. Make a note of any outlines which you cannot read, or which cause you to hesitate.

2   Drill those outlines.

3   Repeat steps 1 and 2 until you can read the passage very quickly and without any hesitation.

4   Take the passage from dictation, by having someone read to you or by recording it yourself on a tape.

5   Repeat the dictation several times but always read through the printed shorthand as quickly as you can before taking the next dictation.

# UNIT 10
## SHUN

The sound of **SHUN** is represented by a large hook or by a small hook (curl).

**The large hook is written:**

Inside curves

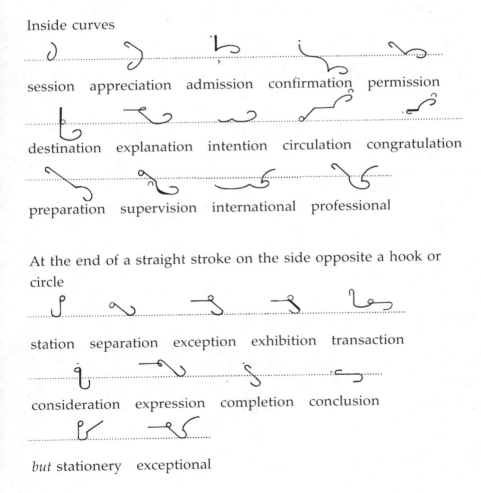

session   appreciation   admission   confirmation   permission

destination   explanation   intention   circulation   congratulation

preparation   supervision   international   professional

At the end of a straight stroke on the side opposite a hook or circle

station   separation   exception   exhibition   transaction

consideration   expression   completion   conclusion

*but* stationery   exceptional

104

On the opposite side to the last vowel

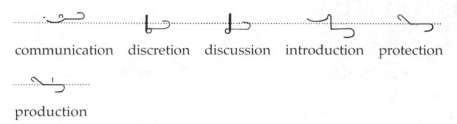

communication  discretion  discussion  introduction  protection

production

Away from the curve formed by **K** or **G** following **F, V, L**

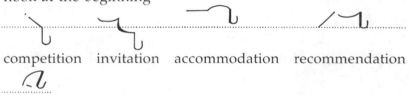

specification  vacation  vocation  delegation  election  selections

On the right side of **T, D, J** when these strokes have no circle or hook at the beginning

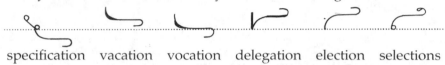

competition  invitation  accommodation  recommendation

logician

**The small SHUN hook is written:**

Following **circle S**, or the **NS circle**, and is represented by a small hook formed by continuing the circle through to the other side of the stroke

conversation  physician  possession  requisition  compensation

**Circle S** may be added by writing a tiny circle inside the hook.
**Stroke L** following the hook may be either joined or disjoined

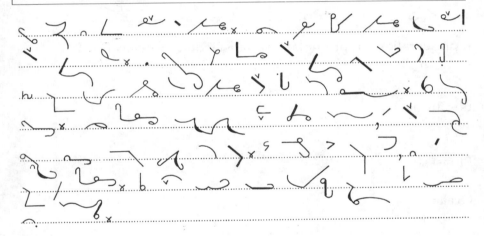

physicians   requisitions   sensational   transitional

**Memo**                                  Homework
**To: Office Manager   From: Chief Accountant**
**Subject: Requisitions**

**Key**

Please ensure you check and sign all requisitions. Some recent /
stationery requisitions have been signed by junior staff. The
preparation / of such documents by juniors should be part of
their / training but you have to take full responsibility for
requisitions / by the addition of your signature. This is for your /
own protection. Most transactions involve quite large sums of

money, / and by careful supervision you can keep within your budget. / With the exception of the petty cash, you ought to / check each transaction. It is my intention to give further / consideration to this matter at the next meeting of managers. /

**(100 words)**

## Short forms

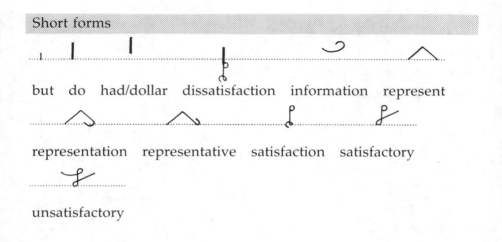

but　do　had/dollar　dissatisfaction　information　represent

representation　representative　satisfaction　satisfactory

unsatisfactory

## Phrases

### Ocean

Atlantic Ocean　Pacific Ocean

(This first phrasing principle is rarely used in business dictation and will not be used in the practice material which follows.)

### Association

your association　Automobile Association　Football Association

Medical Association    trade association

## Intersection

T ⌐ **attention**

## Short form and phrasing drill

**Letter to members of the City Trade Association** HOMEWORK

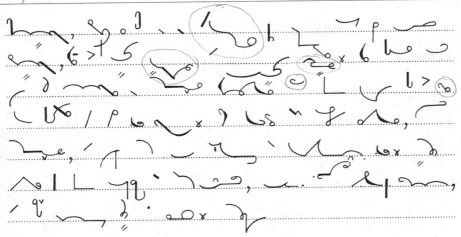

## Key

Dear Member, Special attention is drawn to two large conferences / due to take place in the city next September, those / of the National Football Association and International Medical Association. This / advance information will assist members to organise themselves in order / to take full advantage of the

opportunities for additional business / which such events bring.
There have been complaints about unsatisfactory / service, lack of
organisation, and little or no notification of / forthcoming events.
Your Association representatives do take into consideration all /
of your communications, including congratulations received from
time to time, / and strive to make the Association a success.
Yours truly /                                            **(100 words)**

## CORRESPONDENCE

Letters to and from the International Medical Association of
Physicians and Surgeons.

### Letter to members of the Association

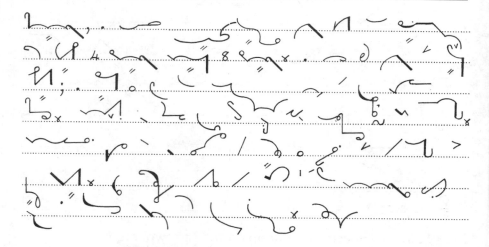

## SKILL DEVELOPMENT

### Getting ready for dictation

1 Check that your notebook is ruled up and that there are enough unused pages.

2 Have a spare pen/pencil ready on the desk. Sharpen pencils in advance.

3 Listen for the first vowel sounds and move your hand into the correct position.

4 Concentrate and listen to the dictation, almost as if it were a story; then, should you have a problem in reading an outline, you will almost certainly be able to remember the word.

5 All strokes are light, but some are lighter than others. Do not press too hard.

6 In examinations do not stop writing, or concentrating, until you hear the dictator announce the end of the examination. The last thing you write is the final full stop or comma.

7 Posture is just as important in shorthand as it is in typewriting. Place your feet firmly on the floor, and let the weight of the body be taken up by leaning on the non-writing arm. Correct posture reduces fatigue.

8 Never write longhand in your notes unless a spelling is given, or unless initials are dictated, such as UN (write such initials in lower case longhand _un._).

## Key

Dear Member, The next International Conference will be held in / Singapore from Thursday 4 September to Monday 8 September. The / main sessions will be on the Friday and Saturday; the / Sunday is free for informal meetings and visits to local / attractions. I am writing to ask you if you plan / to attend and what instructions you have about accommodation. I / am enclosing details of 2 hotels which your Association is / using on the recommendation of the Tourist Board. These very / satisfactory rates are also on offer to members wishing to / have a vacation before or after the conference. Yours sincerely /

**(100 words)**

## Letter to the Secretary of the Association

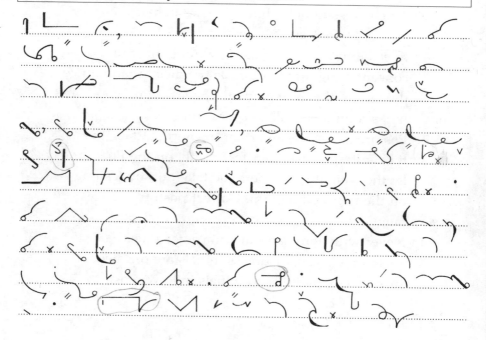

## Key

Dear Dr Lowe, I am delighted that your Association has / taken the decision to use our hotel facilities for your / next conference. From your recent communication I understand that some / of your delegation require accommodation in our associate hotel. As / soon as you have information about final numbers, please advise / our Conference Manager, Mr Stevenson. Mr Stevenson has been appointed / to take charge of our conference clients and is a / man of quite exceptional talents. I guarantee that you will / be impressed by his dedication and I can assure you / of complete satisfaction. A hotel representative will meet your members / at the airport and bring them to their hotel. Please / advise your members they may stay for additional days before / or after the Conference at the special rates. The Hotel / extends an invitation to you and your members to a / cocktail party on the night of your arrival. Yours sincerely /      **(150 words)**

HOMEWORK.

## Letter to the Conference Manager, Singapore International Hotel

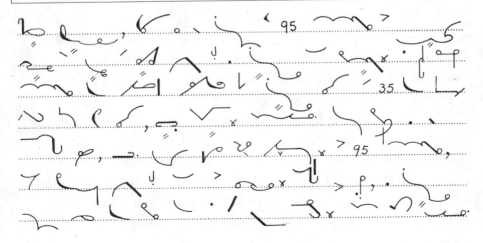

112

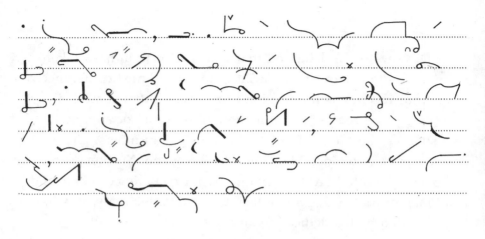

**Key**

Dear Mr Stevenson, This letter is to confirm that ninety– / five members of the International Medical Association of Physicians and / Surgeons will be attending the Conference in September. A total / of 60 members have requested reservations at the Conference hotel / and 35 have taken the option on your other / hotel, Green Park. I am enclosing for your special attention / the 2 accommodation lists, giving full details of what is / required. Of the 95 members, only 70 will be / attending any of the seminars. In addition to the seating, / the Conference room must have space for a large book / exhibition. I am also enclosing a Conference Programme, giving the / times of formal lectures and discussion groups and the refreshment / breaks for each morning and afternoon. After some discussion, a / decision has been reached that members will make their own / arrangements for lunch each day. The Conference Dinner will be / on the Saturday and, with the exception of 5 people, / all members will attend that event. In conclusion let me / say we are looking forward to visiting Singapore. Yours sincerely / **(180 words)**

## SPEED DEVELOPMENT

Turn to page 108 and the passage which begins, *'Dear Member, The next . . .'.*

This passage contains 100 words.

### Your aim

To be able to read and write each outline without hesitation.

### Your action

1 Read through the letter and circle with a pencil any outline which causes you to hesitate.
2 Check each encircled outline with the key.
3 Drill these outlines (refer to page vi to see what drilling really means).
4 Re-read the letter several times until you can read it completely without any hesitation. This is the test. When you can do this it means you do know the outlines.
5 Take the letter from dictation. Which outlines caused you to hesitate when taking the dictation? Identify these by re-reading the printed shorthand and then drill those outlines. Repeat the dictation at least three times.

# UNIT 11
## Prefixes and suffixes

Prefixes are the beginnings of words; suffixes are the endings of words.

## CON/COM/CUM/COG

When the sound **CON–/COM–** begins a word it is represented by a light dot. The vowel sound which follows **CON-, COM-** determines the position of the outline:

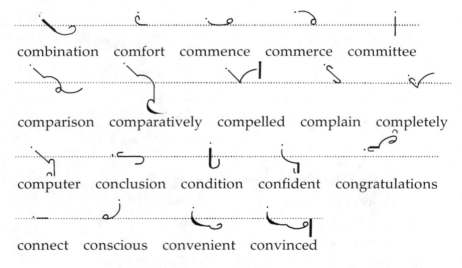

combination   comfort   commence   commerce   committee

comparison   comparatively   compelled   complain   completely

computer   conclusion   condition   confident   congratulations

connect   conscious   convenient   convinced

**CON, COM, CUM, COG** in the middle of a word are represented by writing two strokes close together and omitting the dot:

discontinue   reconsider   recommendation   circumference

recognition   **Note:** I have (come to the) conclusion

## Negative words

Outlines for many negative words are formed by adding stroke
**M**, **L**, **N** or **R** to the beginning of the outline:

immaterial   immoral 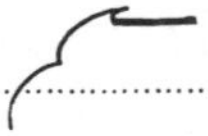  illegal   unnecessary   unknown 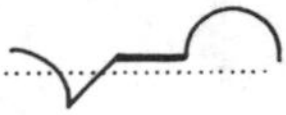  irregular

irrelevant

## -SHIP

This suffix is represented by joined or disjoined stroke **SH**

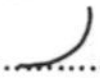

ownership   salesmanship 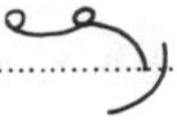  censorship  friendship 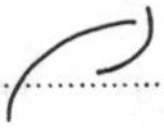  leadership

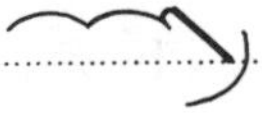

membership

Theory revision drill

**Memo**
**To: Club Treasurer   From: Chairman**
**Subject: Annual fee**

*HOMEWORK.*

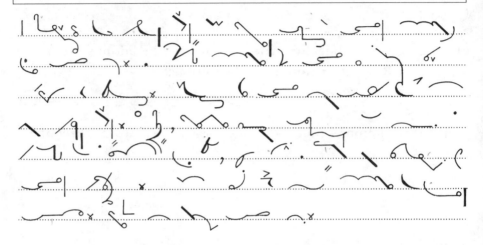

**Key**

It transpires complaints have been received by the Committee about / the proposed <u>introduction</u> of increased membership fees next year. The / <u>majority</u> of members say the increase is <u>comparatively</u> high and / completely <u>without</u> justification. I have come to the conclusion this / increase may be unnecessary and the matter should be reconsidered / by the Committee. As Treasurer, perhaps you can be instrumental / in making a recommendation for a smaller fee adjustment, still / allowing the Club to be self-supporting <u>through</u> increased refreshment / charges. I am conscious <u>of the fact that</u> many members / have fixed incomes. Please contact me before the next meeting. /

**(100 words)**

## Short forms

commercial/commercially  different/difference  differently  of

oh/owe  on  ought  hour/our  ourselves  we  which  who

with

## Phrases

**CON/COM** may be indicated in the middle of a phrase by
writing two outlines close to each other:

I am completely   I will be compelled   I am confident

income tax   lack of confidence   strong competition

I have (come to the) conclusion

**Note:** This rule does not apply to downward short forms and the
short forms **the** and **a**:

to complete   the committee

## Intersection

K ——— company

## Short form and phrasing drill

### Letter to Miss J Common from R Hunter, solicitor

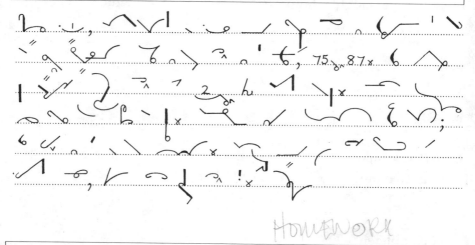

### Key

Dear Miss Common, I will be compelled to <u>commence</u> court /
<u>proceedings</u> <u>against</u> you this week on behalf of <u>Super</u> <u>Sports</u> /
Company Limited <u>unless</u> you pay the <u>amount</u> you owe this /
company, £75.87. This <u>represents</u> the difference / <u>between</u> the
<u>original</u> <u>account</u> and the £200 which / you have already paid.
<u>Commercial</u> firms must press for settlement / of debts. I expect
you are <u>familiar</u> with this <u>policy;</u> / that is why you ought to pay
immediately. I am / confident the Court will grant the <u>application</u>
and award costs, / which will more than <u>double</u> the <u>amount</u>
owing. Yours truly /

**(100 words)**

# SKILL DEVELOPMENT

## Transcription

1 In an examination use the interval between passages to read through the notes just taken.

2 When reading through your notes do not change outlines; make corrections in the margin.

3 In the office take advantage of any interruptions, such as a telephone call, to read through your notes, and always be ready to read back the last two or three sentences before dictation resumes.

4 When the dictation has ended, and before beginning transcription, check through your notes. Take particular notice of any instructions given in the dictation which might affect the work you are about to begin: for example, if a particular document has to be given priority in transcription, even though it was not dictated first; or one letter needs additional copies.

5 As you transcribe, tick each page.

6 Check your transcript against your notes, line by line, outline by outline.

7 Is the transcript mailable? 'Mailable' means correct in every aspect – facts, grammar, spelling and punctuation. Use a dictionary to check for misspellings.

8 If a sentence does not make sense, something must be wrong; recheck your notes.

## CORRESPONDENCE

A memo and two letters from the Television and Electronics Co Ltd.

---

**Memo**

**To: Branch Manager   From: Managing Director**

**Subject: Annual Sales Results**

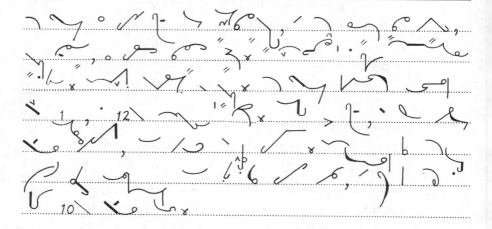

---

**Key**

---

Your branch has won the trophy for the Annual Sales / Competition, and your Senior Sales Representative, Peter Lawson, is once / again Salesman of the Year. My congratulations on a truly / magnificent achievement. I am writing personally to Peter. Your branch / turnover increased by £100,000, a 12 per / cent improvement on last year. In addition to the trophy, / all staff receive the bonus reward, in recognition of outstanding / work. I am convinced it is your confident leadership which / has been instrumental in achieving this wonderful result, and therefore / it earns an additional 10 per cent bonus for you. / **(100 words)**

---

**Letter to Peter Lawson, Senior Sales Representative, South East Branch**

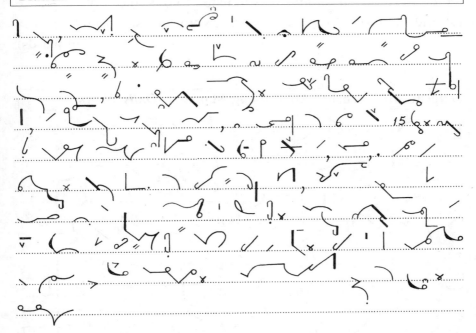

---

**Key**

Dear Peter, I am writing to offer my congratulations on / being made Television and Electronics Company Salesman of the Year. / This is the second time you have won since the / scheme was introduced 4 years ago, which is a superb / accomplishment. In spite of the transport problems which the company / had, and strong competition in the computer market, you increased / your sales by £15,000. You have been achieving / personal monthly

122

targets above those set by the company and, / of course, the results are self-evident. Before taking your / well-earned holiday, I would like you to speak at / the next meeting of Departmental Managers on staff training. I / am confident you will be able to instruct and guide / them on the sort of training policy we should adopt. / We owe it to ourselves to listen to the voice / of experience. I look forward to hearing your views. Sincerely

**(150 words)**

## Letter to Mr J Crosby, Advertising Manager, *Daily News*

## Key

Dear Mr Crosby, I am writing to thank you for / your hard work on behalf of my company. You are / to be congratulated for the efficient manner in which you / handled our recent advertising campaign. I am delighted to inform / you that an announcement has just been made that this / branch was awarded the two top sales prizes. The majority / of our advertising was with your paper and I thought / you would like to share our good news. You were, / of course, instrumental in persuading me to use your Sunday / paper as well as the daily edition, and I am / convinced this combination produced a large percentage of our extra / sales. We ought to get together soon, perhaps one lunch / hour, and set ourselves targets for the next campaign. I / have a tight advertising budget of £22,000 / for this branch, a 10 per cent increase on last / year. I am compelled to obtain the maximum coverage for / this budget, and I hope you are able to recommend / a different, equally successful, scheme at discount rates. Yours sincerely /                                    **(180 words)**

## SPEED DEVELOPMENT

Turn to page 118 and the passage which begins, *'Dear Miss Common, . . .'*. This letter contains many examples of the theory being reviewed in this unit. Some of the outlines will be new to you. Spend as much time as it takes you to learn the new outlines.

### Your aim

To master new outlines through rapid reading.

### Your action

First of all, turn to page vi *'How to use this book'* and read paragraph 3. Follow these instructions whenever rapid reading is mentioned.

1 Rapid read the letter, checking the key if necessary.
2 Repeat this reading until all points of hesitancy have been removed.
3 Take the letter from dictation at least 3 times. Make the most of a cassette player if you have one, or persuade someone to dictate to you by reading from the key. In between each dictation, rapid read the printed shorthand.

# UNIT 12
## KW, GW, WH, and SW

## KW, GW

A large hook at the beginning of strokes **K** and **G** adds **W**. **Circle S** is written inside the hook:

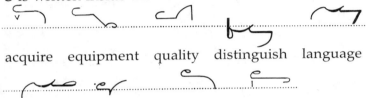

acquire   equipment   quality   distinguish   language

linguist   consequently   square   squander

## WH

**WH** is represented by the sign ⟋ . Although the **H** part of the **WH** sound is not often pronounced, it is always represented in the outline:

why   what   wheels   whilst   meanwhile   worthwhile

## SW

**SW** is represented by writing a tiny **circle S** inside stroke **W**

sway   sweet   swell   swift   swing   switch   persuade

HOMEWORK.

## Letter from the Managing Director, Quality Repairs Limited

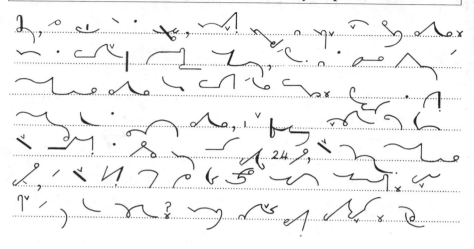

## Key

Dear Sir, As the owner of a new business, I / am writing to persuade you to try my special service. / I am a qualified electrical engineer, offering you a first- / class repair and maintenance service for all quality office equipment. / Frequently the leading manufacturers have a similar service, but I / distinguish myself from them by guaranteeing a response to your / call within 24 hours, by removing maintenance worries, and / by charging much less than the national companies anywhere in / the country. Why not try and see for yourself? I / am sure you will find switching worth while. Yours faithfully /

**(100 words)**

## Short forms

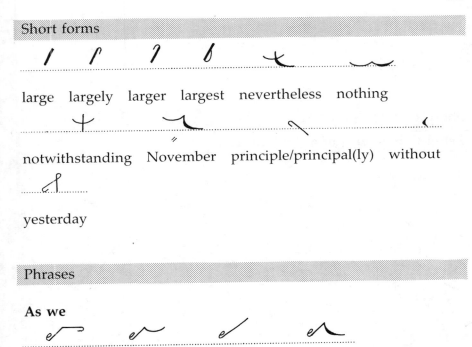

large   largely   larger   largest   nevertheless   nothing

notwithstanding   November   principle/principal(ly)   without

yesterday

## Phrases

**As we**

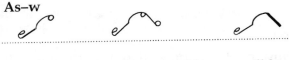

as we can    as we know    as we are    as we have

**As–w**

as well as    as well as possible    as will be

**As–s**

as soon as    as soon as possible    as soon as we can

## Intersection

CH ...⁄... charge

## Short form and phrasing drill

**Letter to members of a Book Society**   HOMEWORK.

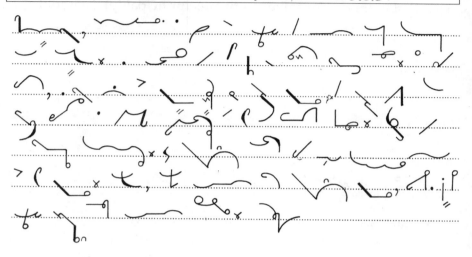

## Key

Dear Member, I am enclosing a list of new charges / which come into effect in November. The increases are largely / due to higher production costs. As you are aware, the / principal aim of the Book Society is to publish books / which people read for pleasure as well as a range / of university and other quality texts. This has been our / practice for many years. Without the popular novel we could / not finance many of the other books. Nevertheless, notwithstanding the / income from popular books, yesterday the Committee set new charges / to produce extra income as soon as possible. Yours truly /

**(100 words)**

## SKILL DEVELOPMENT

### Practise daily

You must give time each day to developing your shorthand skill. Aim to practise for at least 1 hour; divide this into 2 sessions of 30 minutes if you feel it is more beneficial.

Your confidence in taking notes will improve through extra practice. Your notes will improve and, as a direct result, your transcription skill will improve.

1 Drill outlines encountered during the day which caused you to hesitate.
2 Rapid-read shorthand material from the textbooks and from your own notes.
3 Take dictation from a member of the family, or a friend. This gives you a variety of voices, which is good preparation for the business world.
4 Take full advantage of the cassette player if you have one. Dictate material used from a textbook in class that day; take the dictation, check the outlines, drill corrections and repeat the dictation. Dictate the homework material.
5 Use your shorthand dictionary and extend your shorthand vocabulary by adding an extra 10 or 20 outlines to those hundreds you already know.
6 Master any short forms and phrases which still cause a hesitancy in reading or writing.

## CORRESPONDENCE

A draft advertisement, memo and extract from the Chairman's
annual report for Office Equipment International plc.

---

### Draft advertisement for new staff

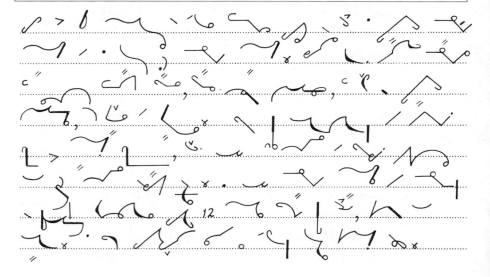

---

### Key

One of the largest manufacturers of office equipment wishes to /
appoint a European Export Manager and a Far East Export /
Manager. As well as having relevant experience with similar
quality / products, applicants must be linguists, with either two
European languages, / or Chinese and Japanese. Principal duties
involved are reporting direct / to the Managing Director, finding
new markets and persuading retailers / in established markets to
switch to this company. The new / Export Managers are expected

131

to distinguish themselves within 12 months / from the date of appointment, which will be in November. / A very worthwhile salary is offered for these challenging posts. / **(100 words)**

---

**Extract from the Chairman's Annual Report**

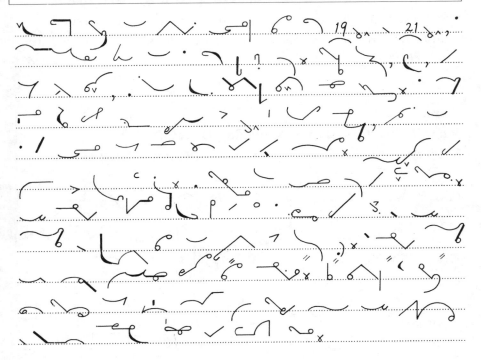

---

**Key**

I have great pleasure in reporting increased sales from nineteen / million pounds to £21 million, a magnificent achievement / in a very difficult trading year. Profits for the year, / however, are only up slightly, the company having absorbed the / higher costs of production. A major cause of this was / the erratic swing of the pound on foreign exchanges, resulting / in a large increase in

132

the cost of some of / our raw materials. Meanwhile we look to the future with / confidence. The prospects for next year are quite promising. New / export targets have been set and as a consequence we / are appointing two new managers to develop sales in Europe / and the Far East. All export managers now must be / linguists as well as sales experts. It is hoped that / special summer promotions in the home market will persuade many / new retailers to become exclusive stockists of our quality products. /

**(150 words)**

**Memo**
**To: All Directors   From: Managing Director**
**Subject: Interviews for appointment of Export Manager**

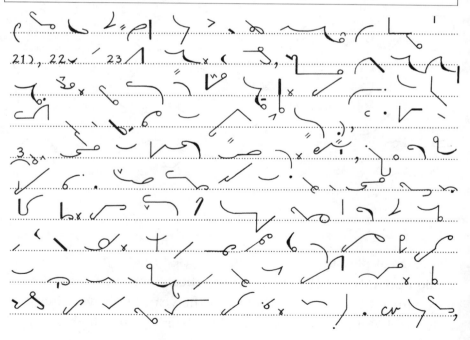

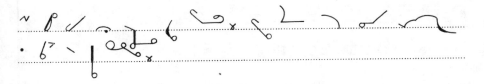

---

**Key**

Three applicants have been short-listed for each of the / two
posts and interviews will take place on 21st, / 22nd and 23rd
November. Without exception, all directors / will be involved in
these appointments. Please clear your diaries / for those dates.
We are looking for top quality people / to boost sales in Europe
and the Far East, with / a target of £3 million increase in turnover
next / year. As we know, competition is very strong but we / are
selling the finest equipment and we are in a / position to increase
production to meet additional demand. We can / acquire larger
factory premises at very short notice should that / be necessary.
Notwithstanding our excellent results this year we must / set the
wheels in motion now to strengthen our position / in the world
markets. It has always been one of / our principles to look well
ahead. I am attaching the / CV for each applicant, and I suggest
we meet / to discuss these applications. Please ask your secretary
to let / me have a choice of dates as soon as possible. / **(180 words)**

## SPEED DEVELOPMENT

Turn to page 130 and the passage which begins 'One of the largest . . .'.

This passage contains 100 words. Many of the outlines are theory examples, short forms and phrases reviewed in this unit.

### Your aim

To take this passage at a speed at least 20 wam above your average.

### Your action

1  Read through the shorthand and identify outlines which cause hesitancy.
2  Drill those outlines until any hesitation is removed.
3  Repeat the reading until you can call it rapid reading.
4  Copy the passage into your notebook, writing quickly and, at the same time, writing accurately.
5  Rapid read the printed shorthand one more time. The material is now totally familiar to you. You now know and can write each outline without any hesitancy.
6  Take the letter from dictation at 20 wam above your average speed. Check outlines. Repeat the dictation. Check outlines and repeat dictation.

# List of short forms

Unit numbers are indicated in brackets.

| | | | |
|---|---|---|---|
| a/an (1) | always (1) | but (10) | |
| accord/ according/ according to (4) | also (1) | cannot (5) | |
| | altogether (1) | character* (7) | |
| | an/a (1) | characteristic* (7) | |
| accord- ingly (4) | and (1) | | |
| acknowledge (3) | any/in (6) | | |
| acknowledg- ment (3) | anybody (6) | commercial -ly (11) | |
| | anyhow (6) | could (5) | |
| advantage* (3) | anyone (6) | | |
| advertise/ -ment* (4) | anything (6) | dear (4) | |
| advertised* (4) | anyway (6) | different/ difference* (11) | |
| advertising* (4) | are (8) | | |
| all (1) | as/has (2) | differently* (11) | |
| almost (1) | | difficult (3) | |
| already (1) | be (1) | difficulty (3) | |
| although (1) | before (4) | disadvantage* (3) | |
| | behalf* (3) | | |

| | | |
|---|---|---|
| dissatisfaction (10) | gentlemen (5) | influence (6) |
| do (10) | had (10) | influential (8) |
| dollar (10) | has/as (2) | information (10) |
| during* (4) | have (3) | insurance* (6) |
| enlarge (6) | his/is (2) | is/his (2) |
| enlargement (6) | hour/our (11) | it (1) |
| enlarger (6) | how (1) | |
| everything* (9) | however* (4) | January (6) |
| eye/I (1) | | |
| | I/eye (1) | knowledge (3) |
| | immediate (5) | knowledge–able (3) |
| February* (3) | immediately (5) | |
| financial-ly* (6) | importance/important* (5) | large (12) |
| first (2) | | largely (12) |
| for (3) | importantly* (5) | larger (12) |
| from (4) | impossible* (2) | largest (12) |
| | in/any (6) | |
| general-ly* (6) | inconvenience –t-ly* (6) | manufacture (7) |
| gentleman (5) | indifferent* (6) | manufacturer (7) |

| | | |
|---|---|---|
| maximum* (7) | our/hour (11) | several (2) |
| minimum* (7) | ourselves (11) | shall (9) |
| misrepresent* (7) | owe/oh (11) | should (9) |
| more (4) | | significance* (9) |
| Mrs (2) | particular (5) | signify/ significant* (9) |
| Ms (2) | particularly (5) | |
| nevertheless (12) | principle/ principal/ principally* (12) | something (9) |
| | | subject (2) |
| nothing (12) | put (9) | sure* (4) |
| notwithstand– ing (12) | | |
| November* (12) | represent* (10) | thank (8) |
| | representation* (10) | thankful (8) |
| number* (4) | | that (8) |
| | representative* (10) | the (1) |
| of (11) | | there/their (7) |
| oh/owe (11) | responsible –ibility (8) | therefore (7) |
| on (11) | | thing (9) |
| | | think (9) |
| opinion* (6) | satisfaction (10) | this (2) |
| opportunity* (5) | satisfactory (10) | to (2) |
| ought (11) | | today (2) |

138

| together (2) | ........—....... | usual/ usually* (1) | ........⌣....... | without (12) | ........⟨....... |
| tomorrow (2) | ........⌄....... | | | wonderful –ly (7) | ........↗....... |
| to be (2) | ........╲....... | very (4) | ........⌐....... | would (9) | ........⌐....... |
| too/two (2) | ........╲....... | | | | |
| toward/ trade (5) | ........η....... | we (11) | ........⟋....... | year (8) | ........⌐....... |
| | | which (11) | ........⟋....... | yesterday (12) | ........⟨....... |
| unsatisfactory (10) | ........⟍....... | who (11) | ........╱....... | you (1) | ........∩....... |
| | | will (8) | ........⟨....... | your (8) | ........⌐....... |
| unusual/ unusually* (1) | ........⟍....... | with (11) | c | yourself (8) | ........⟿....... |

*These are new short forms in Pitman 2000.

# List of Intersections

Unit numbers are indicated in brackets.

arrange/
arranged/
arrangement
(8)

arranging
(8)

attention
(10)

business (2)

charge (12)

company
(11)

company
limited (3)

corporation (9)

department (1)

enquire/
inquire/
enquiry/
inquiry (6)

form (3)

limited (3)

month (5)

morning* (7)

require/
required/
requirement
(4)

*This is a new intersection in Pitman 2000.

# List of 700 Common Words

These outlines represent approximately 68 per cent of the words contained in ordinary English matter*.

| | | | |
|---|---|---|---|
| a | age | another | |
| able | ago | answer | |
| about | agree | any | |
| above | air | appear | |
| according | all | April | |
| account | along | are | |
| across | also | arm | |
| act | altogether | art | |
| add | am | as | |
| advantage | among | ask | |
| advertise advertisement | amount | at | |
| after | an | attempt | |
| afternoon | and | attention | |
| again | animal | August | |
| | announce | authority | |

* Together with their derivative outlines, these words represent approximately 80 per cent of the words in ordinary English matter.

| away | | beyond | | business | |
| | | big | | but | |
| baby | | black | | buy | |
| back | | blue | | by | |
| bad | | board | | bye | |
| balance | | body | | call | |
| bank | | book | | came | |
| base | | both | | can | |
| be | | bought | | capital | |
| beautiful | | boy | | car | |
| because | | brake | | care | |
| become | | bread | | carry | |
| bed | | break | | case | |
| before | | bring | | cause | |
| begin | | brother | | cell | |
| behind | | brought | | certain | |
| belief | | build | | change | |
| believe | | building | | character | |
| best | | built | | charge | |
| better | | buoy | | cheap | |
| between | | burn | | check | |
| | | | | cheque | |

|  |  |  |
|------|------|------|
| chief | control | depend |
| child | copy | desire |
| children | cost | detail |
| city | could | develop |
| clean | country | die |
| clear | course | differ |
| coal | cover | difference difference |
| coarse | credit | different |
| cold | cry | difficult |
| colour | custom | difficulty |
| come | cut | direct |
| comfort | | discover |
| commit | danger | distance |
| common | date | distribute |
| company | day | division |
| competition | dear | do |
| complete | December | door |
| condition | deep | doubt |
| connect | degree | down |
| consider | deliver | dress |
| continue | demand | drink |
| | | drive |

| | | |
|---|---|---|
| during | event | February |
| dye | ever | feel |
| | every | few |
| each | example | field |
| early | except | figure |
| earth | exchange | final |
| ease | exist | find |
| east | expect | fire |
| education | experience | first |
| effect | expert | fish |
| either | express | fly |
| electric | eye | follow |
| electricity | | food |
| employ | face | foot |
| end | fact | for |
| engine | fall | force |
| engineer | family | form |
| English | far | forward |
| enough | farm | free |
| equal | father | frequent |
| even | fear | Friday |

| | | | |
|---|---|---|---|
| friend | grow | high | |
| from | him | | |
| front | had | himself | |
| full | half | his | |
| fully | hand | history | |
| further | happen | hold | |
| future | happy | hole | |
| | hard | home | |
| gave | has | hope | |
| general generally | have | horse | |
| | he | hour | |
| gentlemen | head | house | |
| get | health | how | |
| girl | hear | however | |
| give | heart | hundred | |
| go | heat | | |
| gold | heavy | I | |
| good | heir | idea | |
| govern | help | if | |
| government | her | immediate | |
| great | here | important importance | |
| ground | | | |

| | | |
|---|---|---|
| impossible | June | left |
| improve | just | less |
| in | | let |
| increase | keep | letter |
| indeed | kind | life |
| industry | king | light |
| influence | knew | like |
| inform | know | limit |
| inform-ation | knowledge | line |
| | | list |
| instruction | labour | little |
| insurance | land | live |
| interest | language | long |
| iron | large | longer |
| is | last | look |
| issue | late | loss |
| it | law | love |
| itself | lead | low |
| | learn | |
| January | least | machine |
| judge | leave | made maid |
| July | | |

146

| | | | | | | |
|---|---|---|---|---|---|---|
| make | | might | | must | |
| man | | mile | | my | |
| manufac-ture | | milk | | myself | |
| many | | million | | | |
| March | | mind | | name | |
| mark | | mine | | nation | |
| market | | minute | | nature | |
| marry | | Miss | | near | |
| mass | | modern | | necessary | |
| master | | moment | | need | |
| matter | | Monday | | neither | |
| may | | money | | never | |
| me | | month | | new | |
| meal | | more | | news | |
| mean | | morning | | next | |
| measure | | most | | night | |
| meat | | mother | | no | |
| meet | | motor | | nor | |
| member | | move | | north | |
| memory | | Mr | | not | |
| method | | much | | note | |

| | | | | |
|---|---|---|---|---|
| nothing | | open | | paper |
| November | | operate | | part |
| now | | opinion | | particular |
| number | | opport-unity | | party |
| | | or | | pass |
| object | | order | | pay |
| observation | | organise | | peace |
| October | | organisation | | pence |
| of | | other | | people |
| off | | ought | | perfect |
| offer | | our | | perhaps |
| office | | ourselves | | person |
| official | | out | | personal |
| often | | over | | picture |
| oh! | | owe | | piece |
| oil | | owing | | place |
| old | | own | | plain |
| on | | | | plan |
| once | | | | plane |
| one | | page | | plant |
| only | | paint | | play |

| | | |
|---|---|---|
| please | purpose | record |
| pleasure | put | red |
| point | | regard |
| political | quality | regret |
| poor | quarter | regular |
| position | question | relate |
| possible | quick | remark |
| pound | quite | remember |
| power | | report |
| present | radio | represent |
| price | rail | require |
| principal | rate | respect |
| principally | rather | respons- |
| principle | reach | ible |
| probable | read | -ibility |
| product | ready | rest |
| profit | real | result |
| property | really | return |
| provide | reason | right |
| public | receive | river |
| publish | recent | road |
| pull | | |

| | | | |
|---|---|---|---|
| room | seen | simple | |
| round | self | since | |
| rule | sell | sir | |
| run | send | sit | |
| | sense | situation | |
| safe | sent | six | |
| said | September | size | |
| sail | serious | small | |
| sale | serve | so | |
| same | service | some | |
| satisfactory | set | sometimes | |
| Saturday | several | soon | |
| save | sew | sort | |
| say | shall | sound | |
| scene | she | south | |
| school | ship | sow | |
| science | short | speak | |
| sea | should | special | |
| second | show | spend | |
| see | side | spent | |
| seem | sign | stand | |

| | | | |
|---|---|---|---|
| start | supply | then | |
| state | support | there | |
| station | sure | therefore | |
| steal | surprise | these | |
| steel | | | |
| step | sweet | they | |
| still | system | thing | |
| | | think | |
| stone | | third | |
| stop | table | this | |
| store | take | those | |
| story | talk | though | |
| straight | tax | thought | |
| strange | teach | thousand | |
| street | tell | through | |
| strong | test | Thursday | |
| subject | than | till | |
| success | thank | time | |
| such | that | | |
| suggest | the | to | |
| sum | their | together | |
| summer | them | told | |
| Sunday | themselves | tomorrow | |

| | | |
|---|---|---|
| too | use | Wednes-day |
| touch | usual usually | week |
| toward | | weigh |
| town | value | well |
| trade | very | went |
| train | view | were |
| tried | voice | west |
| trouble | | what |
| true | waist | whatever |
| trust | walk | when |
| truth | want | whenever |
| try | war | where |
| Tuesday | warm | whether |
| turn | was | which |
| two | waste | while |
| | watch | white |
| under | water | who |
| until | way | whole |
| up | we | whom |
| upon | weak | whose |
| us | weather | why |

| | | | | | |
|---|---|---|---|---|---|
| wide | | wonderful | | wrong | |
| will | | wonder-fully | | | |
| window | | word | | yard | |
| winter | | work | | year | |
| wire | | world | | yes | |
| wise | | worth | | yesterday | |
| wish | | would | | yet | |
| with | | wrest | | you | |
| within | | write | | young | |
| without | | writer | | your | |
| woman | | writing | | | |
| women | | written | | | |